PERILOUS TIDES
Real-Life Stories from Knik, Alaska

Table of Contents

DEDICATION

This book is dedicated to those who find themselves struggling through the storms and perilous tides of life. If you feel like you're sinking, with no hope in sight, then this book is for you!

ACKNOWLEDGEMENTS

I would like to thank Duane Guisinger for his vision for this book and MaryKay Shively for her hard work in making it a reality. And to the people of Sunny Knik, thank you for your boldness and vulnerability in sharing your personal stories.

This book would not have been published without the amazing efforts of our project manager and editor, Hayley Pandolph. Her untiring resolve pushed this project forward and turned it into a stunning victory. Thank you for your great fortitude and diligence. Deep thanks to our incredible Editor in Chief, Michelle Cuthrell, and Executive Editor, Jen Genovesi, for all the amazing work they do. I would also like to thank our invaluable proofreader, Melody Davis, for the focus and energy she has put into perfecting our words.

Lastly, I want to extend our gratitude to the creative and very talented Jenny Randle, who designed the beautiful cover for *Perilous Tides: Real-Life Stories from Knik, Alaska.*

Daren Lindley
President and CEO
Good Catch Publishing

The book you are about to read
is a compilation of authentic life stories.
The facts are true, and the events are real.
These storytellers have dealt with crisis, tragedy, abuse
and neglect and have shared their most private moments,
mess-ups and hang-ups in order for others to learn and
grow from them. In order to protect the identities of those
involved in their pasts, the names and details of some
storytellers have been withheld or changed.

INTRODUCTION

Life isn't always smooth sailing. It's easy to feel like you're on top of the world and suddenly find that everything in your life has come to a grinding halt. You find yourself sinking into a nightmare you didn't see coming. Perhaps, for you, life has been full of incredible hurt, abuse, abandonment, denial, disappointment or fear. Maybe you wake up every morning gripped by your addiction to some substance or behavior. Maybe you think, *There is no way out of this!* Each day brings a growing awareness of impending hopelessness and destructive guilt. Slipping ever deeper, you feel the perilous tides rising, from which you're sure there is no return.

Your life really can change. It is possible to become a new person. The seven stories you are about to read prove positively that people right here in our community have stopped dying and started living. Whether they've been beaten by abuse, broken promises, shattered dreams or suffocating addictions, the resounding answer is, "Yes! You can become a new person." The potential to break free from gloom and into a bright future awaits.

Expect inspiration, hope and transformation! As you walk with people from our very own area through the pages of this book, you will not only find riveting accounts of their hardships, you will learn the secrets that brought about their breakthroughs. These people are no longer living in the shadows of yesterday; they are thriving with a sense of mission and purpose TODAY. May these stories inspire you to do the same.

THE FATE OF THE MARINER
The Story of Eldon Gallear
Written by Richard Drebert

Commander Walther Kolle lined up periscope crosshairs on the SS *Tillie Lykes* amidships.

"Torpedo LOS!"

U-boat 154 shimmied as the projectile sped toward the enemy's perfect silhouette against a gray morning haze. The German submarine commander shifted his weight to one black boot, willing his torpedo a little *north*, but the explosive lance detonated slightly astern of the freighter's midsection — a few feet aft of his intended mark.

Kolle swore under his breath. He had intended to pierce the ship's engine room dead-center.

At 3:48 a.m., the *Tillie Lykes* sucked ocean into a jagged maw, and flames engulfed the wheelhouse where Kolle imagined the shipmaster met his end. Kolle's kill moaned as steam lines ruptured and spat white vapors into the air. He scanned the sinking vessel with his periscope fore and aft, transfixed by the freighter's death throes. Of course, no sailor working or sleeping in the belly of the ship survived — but dozens of deckhands typically scurried like ants, trying to leap over rails before the ocean swallowed iron and flesh.

This old freighter seemed resigned to its death; only three figures stood at a rail of the listing deck, and below them a single floating life raft bumped the side of the doomed cargo ship. Rivets popped from heat, and the *Tillie's* iron bow split from the stern, ripping the wound wider. Captain Kolle cursed again as he tried to identify the freighter, but he couldn't see its name in the dawn's half-light. Suddenly the *Tillie* plunged beneath the waves like two halves of a steel barrel. Ignited oil roiled with the ocean swells, and the Nazi commander marked his journal: *Direct hit; 18 seconds until torpedo impact; two minutes and 30 seconds to sink.*

Kolle ordered his submarine crew to surface, vexed at his target's lack of military courtesy. Obviously the freighter was one of America's defenseless merchant ships, but Kolle's peers might question his ambush if he failed to deliver the name of the vessel.

The commander climbed to the open bridge above the conning tower. Sultry gray swells rolled between U-boat 154 and a flimsy canvas-clad life raft. Five men lay or clung to the wood slats lashed between its leaky pontoons, and he hollered his best English over the roaring wind and slapping waves.

"What is your ship? Name! What name?"

Only one man on the raft spoke English — and I was barely conscious. I bled from a deep wound in my side. The other sailors shrugged, waved and cried for help in Portuguese.

German U-boat Commander Walther Kolle descended his conning tower and set a course for another kill, leaving us bobbing amid debris and bodies.

THE FATE OF THE MARINER

৵৵৵

I was 17, cleaning cow barns and repairing tractors on my dad's dairy farm the day the Japanese bombed Pearl Harbor. Adolf Hitler declared war on the United States four days after the Pearl attack, and Nazi Admiral Karl Donitz launched Operation Drum Beat — a long-ranging scheme to sink every merchant ship supplying arms, fuel and food to Allied troops.

With only 21 weapons-ready unterseebootes (submarines), Donitz ravaged the shipping lanes of Britain and the United States, while Hitler ordered hundreds of subs mass produced at Bremen. Seamen called these merciless ship killers U-boats, and Germany soon controlled Atlantic and Pacific cargo routes with their wolf packs.

Blame Captain Jim for my obsession with ships and faraway places. My aunt Gertie, Dad's youngest sister, married Captain Jim Barber, retired master of a fuel tender who sailed the Inside Passage from Seattle. When I was near 13, middle-aged Jim and Gertie honeymooned at our dairy farm, and with big round eyes I plied Gertie's captain with questions at my father's grand oak table. Our big Federal woodstove (and my father's homebrew) warmed the mariner and his audience as Captain Jim roared about monster swells he rode on a freighter rounding the Horn of Africa.

"Eldon, I tell ya's, those black mountains never broke

like normal waves, because no islands nor continents stood in their way. They rolled on and on like a thousand miles of African sand dunes. And that's the way a man should live, m'lad! With nothing in his way!"

I was never the same after the captain's honeymoon at the Gallear family farm. I dreamed of escaping manure and milking machines, and Dad's hope that I might stay and help make the farm profitable drifted out to sea.

My grandpa, Samuel Curry, Mom's father, had emigrated from Northern Ireland. He labored as a boilermaker back East until working his way west. My grandmother, Lizzie, sailed away from Central Ireland to South America around the time of the Great Potato Famine. She traveled by mule through Panama, then sailed up the coast to Port Townsend, Washington.

Grandpa Sam married my grandmother, Lizzie, and homesteaded in the Chimacum Valley, until they nearly lost the farm during the Great Depression.

Grandpa and Grandma Gallear had emigrated from England and homesteaded at Yelm (195 miles from Chimacum), and Dad was one of 14 children. My mother, Marguerite, grew up at Chimacum and taught school there. She married my father, Albert Gallear, and together they settled at Yelm until opportunity knocked.

I was 5 years old when Dad loaded two Model T Fords with our belongings to settle at Grandpa Curry's farm at Chimacum. Throughout the Depression, Dad worked side jobs all over the county to save my grandpa from the bankers. Later my father bought the Curry farm and, in time, squirreled away enough from harvesting canning peas, acres of sugar beets and other crops to buy dairy cows.

"Eldon! Get your a** outta bed, and get those cows in the barn!" (Dad's barn-holler is still echoing in my brain 80 years later!).

At 4:30 a.m., my feet hit the cold wood, and I hoped that the old two-cylinder milking machine wouldn't hiccup before the last cow was finished. After calling in our 40 Guernseys and Jerseys and washing 160 teats, it was my job to tinker and tweak the machine morning and evening to keep milk flowing to the tank.

"Eldon. Don't you let that contraption die on us, or we'll be milking by hand …"

I *hated* cows — but unbeknownst to my father, he was planting a *passion* for machinery in my mind. I lived and breathed pistons, crankshafts, spark plugs — and later, massive boilers and steam engines propelling multi-ton freighters.

When local farmers learned about Chimacum's 12-year-old mechanical prodigy, my father faced stiff competition for my time.

"If that boy can keep ol' Gallear's '26 Fordson tractor limping across his fields, he can fix d*** near anything!"

Dad grudgingly loaned me out; it was the neighborly thing to do.

I graduated from high school (under threat of death) and left our farm while my mother wept and my father cussed. They were shorthanded now, even with my two brothers and two sisters. I escaped to the docks of Seattle and applied for duty on the SS *Shasta*, a 216-foot ferry serving Port Ludlow and Edmonds, Washington.

At 5 feet, 8 inches and 175 pounds, I was built for hard work, and the engineers aboard the *Shasta* gave me the job known in every trade as "go-fer."

It seemed to be an answer to my prayers as I threw down my sea bag in the firemen's quarters, with coarse men of the sea like Uncle Jim. All my growing-up years my dear mother and Grandma Curry insisted that us Gallear kids attend the Methodist church for Sunday school. And the day the *Shasta* departed Seattle, I figured I was pretty close to heaven.

"Get your a** out of that bunk, and grab some grub, kid!"

It wasn't my father's voice — and a peach-fuzz grin stole over my face. My bare feet hit the deck — this time *iron* cold. I followed my shipmates to the galley and swallowed hard biscuits before my first exciting day below decks in the humid, thunderous engine room.

Steam belched from escape valves. Massive pistons slapped inside steam cylinders powered by blackened burners drinking barrels of crude oil. Inside the *Shasta's* noisy belly, I aspired to one day be a steamship fireman — one of those dependable men who controlled the steam pressure ordered by the ship's master in the wheelhouse above. It took me two separate ferries to run the gamut from wiper (cleaning up messes) to water tender (supplying water to steam boilers) and oiler (lubing engine parts). Helpful engineers pegged me as a full-fledged fireman on a Puget ferry someday, but I knew that it was just a matter of time before I tossed my sea bag aboard an ocean-bound ship.

I bid farewell to my companions on my second ferry, Seattle's SS *Iroquois*, confident in my abilities to land a job in any engine room. I planned to work from the bottom, just like I had on the ferries — but this time aboard the SS *William L. Thompson*, my first freighter.

At 18, I proudly carried documents proving I was a U.S. Merchant Mariner, serving my country. We had no merchant mariner's uniforms in those days, only dungarees, white chambray shirts, shined boots and a hat of our choice. I had leaped from the farm to engine rooms, and I adopted the opinions of seamen who remembered the horrors of World War I — the d*** Huns were at it again …

Cargo ships on the Pacific Coast had been requisitioned to haul fuel, freight and troops wherever the Navy commanded captains to go. The SS *Thompson* (built in 1917 for World War I in Scotland and fondly called The Long Time Tommy for being one of the slowest ships in the fleet) now served the tiny harbors along Alaska's Inside Passage, the same route Uncle Jim had sailed.

But, as I stepped upon the gangplank of the Long Time Tommy, I frowned at a more immediate problem than German gun boats. Stories of the *Thompson's* bully had fouled our galley on the *Iroquois,* like smoke from a dirty stack.

"He's a bully to the *Thompson's* whole crew, and he feeds on young meat, Eldon. Beware!"

I hoped that the brute worked above decks, leaving us firemen to do our jobs in peace.

Maybe we would never even meet ...

A few minutes before 8 a.m., I stepped off the gangplank into cold morning shadows aboard the *William L. Thompson* to report for duty. My duffle weighed down one shoulder, and suddenly a voice scraped my hopes raw.

"Hey, boy."

The brute stood a head taller than me as he shuffled into the sunlight, and I blinked hard to focus on his sneer. I tossed my sea bag on the deck and glanced toward my destination, the bridge, where the captain waited. But not a soul stirred anywhere.

"The name's Bruno, and you'll get to know me. I'm top dog aboard the *Thompson*; I say jump, and you say how high. I run this tub."

It took me just a second or two to gather my wits for an answer. I was an artist at quick comebacks, often defusing a tongue lashing or thrashing from my dad.

"Does that include our master and the mates?" I asked respectfully and set my boots flatfooted on the deck, turning sideways a bit.

"They're like you — all a bunch of candy-a****..."

It was enough. I knew the pecking order by heart as a U.S. Merchant Mariner. I was a seaman and no d*** patsy.

I reached low, about the elevation of my crotch, then stroked upward like a steam piston against his jaw, lifting him to his toes. He flopped to the steel deck like a limp cod and lay still by my sea bag. Blood oozed from his mouth, and I glanced at his broken teeth as I stepped over him to report for duty.

A couple cronies collected the brute later, but they couldn't find a hunk of his severed tongue. I never met the bully again, and no one messed with the engine room crew on our 10-month voyage supplying fuel and equipment to troops digging in on the Aleutian Islands.

I've always felt sorry about my youthful indiscretion, but in the grand schematics of life, perhaps I saved my shipmate. It's hard to take a bully seriously if he talks with a lisp. And just maybe it shamed him away from mouthing off to a sailor wielding a sharpened marlin spike.

Aboard the Long Time Tommy, I dogged the steps of the engineers and fastened their skills to my brain. I polished my aptitude to a blinding sheen and soon advanced to water tender.

Friendships are often made for life aboard a vessel, and mine, with the Poet of Long Time Tommy, will last into eternity — though we parted and never laid eyes on each other again.

He was an able-bodied seaman, and one day out of the blue, our poet, Tom, read me like a book: "Eldon. You don't drink or carouse much."

"Nah," I said, "I weren't taught that way back home. I was raised on a dairy farm in Chimacum, Washington."

I felt a twinge of homesickness for my father and

mother as I described my family and childhood and how I ran off to sea.

"I'm from Seattle," Tom said and grinned. "Good to see you were raised by Christian folk. Say, give me a few days, and I'll write you a poem."

And he did. His words unfurled like a ship's sail, describing my young life at sea and what home really means.

అ~అ~అ

Boom, boom, boom ...

The drum beat a deadly cadence. I stood at the rail of the SS *Island Maiden* at a port off the coast of South America, watching sweating, bronze-skinned men lining the dock shoulder to shoulder, beginning at a warehouse two ball fields away. The human conveyor belt snaked aboard our ship and down into the *Maiden's* dark hold, where green bananas were stacked by the ton.

Suddenly, the drum stopped. A single 125-pound banana stalk slipped from one man's grasp, and he crumpled to the dock as husky natives kicked and beat him unmercifully. When he stopped screaming, the drums resumed their cadence. Another native stepped in line to fill the bloodied banana handler's place.

The workers were paid 10 cents a day, and we loaded 7,000 tons of green bananas in less than 48 hours. Aboard the *Island Maiden*, I worked in the engine room as an oiler, and like all merchant seamen, I was required to sign ship's articles promising that I would sail to our destination and back to the United States port. We left South America for Galveston, Texas, where I expected to collect $110 for my month below decks tending the *Maiden's* engines.

My mother had instilled in me that a man was made in the image of God and that life was precious, but in foreign ports and sometimes even aboard ship, reality ran cross-grained to my young convictions.

One vicious captain I sailed with from Manila never made port in San Francisco. Nobody knew where he went — officially. But the crew had an inkling. He was no d*** good and somehow fell overboard after arguing with an iron pipe. A master could be testy, but not cruel and unreasonable if he wanted to maintain his crew's respect.

At Galveston I waited aboard the *Maiden* for two days, waiting for pay that never came. I went ashore and met two other merchant seaman.

"The *Tillie Lykes* is about to sail to the Caribbean. She's shorthanded, I hear …"

That was enough for me, and I grabbed the first cabbie I could find who knew where she docked. I no sooner hopped off the gang plank than the engineer fastened his beefy fingers on my arm and asked my line of work.

"Fireman, sir." I grinned, and down we went to the engine room 30 feet below decks. The *Tillie* was a demanding, cantankerous old gal, and the fireman I replaced was *done* with her. His eyes looked like two pee-holes in a snow bank, and he couldn't wait to shove off.

The engineer was so frazzled that he forgot to give me ship's articles to sign, and I didn't insist. I just went to work — a ghost learning the tics and twitches of old *Tillie* as she gathered steam to leave Galveston. We were bound for Puerto Rico, and formal paperwork wouldn't have mattered, anyway, since no Coast Guard or Navy ship even bothered to search for a scrap of the old bulker — or her 30 merchant sailors who they thought had vanished without a trace.

"We're after a short load of bauxite to make aluminum for our planes," our engineer told us as we rumbled across open seas toward Puerto Rico.

I had no idea that Nazi U-boats infested the Caribbean like wasps on fresh meat. Our Captain, Gus Darnell, zigzagged a worried course at varying speeds to confuse undersea navigators studying American shipping lanes. Darnell's last ship, the *Cardonia* (also unarmed), had been shelled by German deck guns off Haiti, and Darnell and his crew had escaped in lifeboats before a U-boat finished off the *Cardonia.*

Everything aboard the *Tillie* seemed put together hastily, including our skeleton crew of Brazilian deckhands who spoke Portuguese with a dash of broken English. And our black gang (engine room workers), a mix of Irishmen and Americans, had no replacement for a single injured or sick fireman.

I hoped that Darnell would fill out our contingent when we docked at Puerto Rico. We ran at full speed ahead morning till night, and night until morning. I had taken the groggy morning watch, and all was well with the pulsating pistons inside the massive ship's cylinders. Six burners roared, and black smoke belched steadily in the *Tillie's* wake. Captain Darnell hadn't changed his orders: Forward. Full Speed. Steam pressure: 200 pounds. Everything seemed skookum, as Uncle Jim used to say.

That June morning our *Tillie Lykes* joined a seafloor graveyard with 336 Allied ships sunk by U-boats in the Caribbean in 1942.

Seconds after the German torpedo hit, I scraped myself off the boiler deck, 30 feet below the ocean surface, dazed and groping for handholds in the pitch black. Yellow sparks flashed, lighting the engine room intermittently. The ship was already listing and vibrating. The *Tillie's* pistons throbbed valiantly for a time before saltwater drowned her boilers.

I found a handrail and stumbled up the companionway, conscious but floating, or carried, or spirited along somehow until I reached the top deck. A few feet from me, men shouted to one another in Portuguese, and I shuffled like a drunk toward their voices. I felt their hands on my shoulders and ciphered words in broken English, "You real hu't bad!"

I came around long enough to feel the cold steel handrail in my fingers and see the roiling ocean 20 feet below. A life raft bobbed at the *Tillie's* rising water line, where two Brazilians motioned excitedly, screaming in a foreign tongue. I left the ship then — in mind and body — belly flopping onto the rolling swells. The two crewmen had tossed me in the drink and saved my bacon.

I regained consciousness, heaving up saltwater, while strong arms hauled me aboard the rickety life raft; they dragged my sopping cohorts, formerly standing at the *Tillie's* handrail, inside, too.

I wasn't aware of the next few moments, as the *Tillie Lykes* succumbed to the waves. My four Brazilians must have rowed quickly away from the freighter before her plunge, or we might have filled the empty wake, chasing our sinking *Tillie* down.

Drifting in and out of consciousness, I recall shouts minutes after the sinking. It must have been the unsatisfying conversation between our savage unterseeboote nemesis, Captain Kolle, and the Brazilians.

There are some things a man never forgets, even after nearly 70 years. My first kiss. My first job aboard the ferry *Shasta.* The confrontation with a bully aboard the *Thompson.* Riding out a tidal wave in the Aleutians.

Sharks.

I was alone in the life raft, and I don't know for how long. My four friends had been rescued by native island fishermen, and I guess they figured I was dead — as much blood as had drained from the gash in my side, between the raft slats and into the ocean.

I hated being conscious to feel the bumps and nudges. Great white sharks gathered in the wake of ocean carnage, and no wounded man survived long in the warm Caribbean. Vultures of the sea cleaned up after every German kill.

Sometimes my raft's canvas pontoon would lift into the air, then slap the ocean surface as a shark tried to roll me off. They seemed frantic in the beginning, smelling my blood in the water. But as my body naturally staunched the stream, the sharks just circled, playfully thumping the slats beneath me.

I believed that I was about to die. I lay like an invertebrate, my muscles spent and limbs feeling like boiled macaroni. The afternoon sun seared my face and bare chest, while I waited for angels to bear me up and away.

They had expedited my climb up the companionway after the torpedo hit the *Tillie* when I was shell-shocked. How else could I have escaped certain death in that engine room — a U-boat captain's textbook sweet spot?

I have no idea how long I cooked in that life raft. I had entered a dream state, unaware that the crew of an anti-sub seaplane rescued me from the circling sharks. The Martin Mariner flew me to Panama, where young Navy doctors seemed anxious to write my obituary. I *was* a mess. Shrapnel had ground into my intestines, and I had little blood left to bleed anymore.

I briefly came to, lying on my back upon a mattress, staring at a dingy ceiling. I felt aware of a figure beside me, and I turned my head to focus upon ... *white stockings*!

Was I in heaven? No — I still felt too much pain.

"Where am I?" I croaked weakly.

"Margarita Hospital," a gentle voice said.

"How did I get here?"

I could hear a smile in her words. "I don't know, but thank goodness you're alive."

"Are you my nurse?"

"No, Eldon. I'm your guardian angel. I hear your nurse coming down the hall."

I turned my head slightly toward footsteps and would have asked more ... but my guardian angel vanished. I passed out again.

While I slept, an elderly family doctor looked me over and upset the consensus of Navy physicians.

"Gentlemen, I believe we can save him."

Sending this old doctor is one more mystifying circumstance that I read in the diagram of my eventful life.

After picking out parts of the *Tillie* from my intestines and removing my shredded appendix, the old healer closed me up.

I awoke after surgery, but my guardian angel hadn't returned. She had been replaced by two soldiers at each end of the room holding M-1 Garand rifles. German POWs filled this recovery station, and I tried to sit up.

"What the h*** am I doing here?"

One armed guard, unsmiling, said, "Nobody knows who you are."

I raised my sunburned arm weakly and flashed my sailor's ID number: 11-738. "This oughta tell you something! I'm a merchant seaman outta Seattle!" I was getting my old vinegar back, and it felt good. Now if I could just get away from all these Krauts.

The next day they transferred me to another ward. Thank God for my tattoo, made-to-order for just such an occasion.

The Red Cross seemed to be in charge of care and communications for hospitalized troops — and they were less than helpful. All I needed was a pencil, paper, envelope and stamp, but these items seemed as rare as fresh cream in a ship's galley. Weeks oozed past as I recovered my strength, and I worried that my survival letter might not beat the inevitable death letter speeding its way to my parents. The Navy would regret to inform my family that all hands aboard the SS *Tillie Lykes* had been lost at sea.

It was more than two weeks before I drafted a Salvation Army nurse to help me get a note off to my folks — too late. My mom had received an official Navy correspondence and couldn't bring herself to tell Dad about losing the son who chose life at sea over milking cows on his Chimacum farm.

At Margarita, in the painful watches of the night, I had little else to do but cogitate upon how and why God spared my life. Like a ship's insistent bell, God's voice tolled deep in my heart, drawing me closer to decision. Finally I knew it was time to set my compass for a new course: to serve this merciful captain forever. God had saved me from sinking with the ship and delivered me from the terrors of circling sharks. Now the *soul within the sailor* embraced Jesus for the first time.

Before I left Panama, I asked Jesus, who in Bible stories walked upon the seas, to drop anchor in my heart, and in my 88 years, he has never left me.

In fretful months ahead, I fought infection *and* military red tape, ending up in a Boston infirmary to heal. A government voucher caught up with me there, and I took a berth aboard a troop train back to Seattle. Then I drove home to see my family at Chimacum. At my father's grand oak table, our tearful reunion shall always be a memory I treasure.

After my experiences in the Caribbean, I began to live as if God had some purpose for my near-death odyssey. I've never been a man to broadcast my faith with a bullhorn, but thereafter, wherever I've labored, my Bible lay in view for all men to see.

ॐ ॐ ॐ

There was no use begging Elaine to change her mind.

She was the first woman I really loved, and she was making me choose between her and my career as a merchant seaman.

I was on a blind date with Peggy, her sister, when Elaine hooked me like a springtime salmon. Wherever I made port, I sent Elaine pictures and letters to impress her.

After the Allies broke up the Nazi wolf packs, I figured

it was safe enough to finally tie the knot, and I proposed.

World War II had ended, but so did my dream.

"You've been good to me, Eldon, but I'll never marry a sailor."

I felt like my ship had sailed without me.

I told the dispatcher to get me on any ship, going anywhere — and I signed on as second engineer aboard the SS *Angoon*, a massive ocean-going tug that hauled barges up and down the Alaska Inside Passage.

Dog Passion Daddy Deals was second mate on the *Angoon*, and after some months nursing my wounded pride, I didn't feel one iota better. Deals (Marvin was his given name) commiserated with me because he had woman troubles, too, but nothing he advised ever made a lick of sense.

We were bound for Anchorage, April Fool's Day, 1946, and I had just finished my watch at 4 a.m. I shuffled up to the wheelhouse with a cup of Joe, when I stopped dead. The bosun (petty officer) and an able-bodied seaman stood like statues pointing toward the bow, with mouths as wide open as coffee cans.

I followed their gazes, and my mouth dropped open, too. The highest wave I ever saw bore down upon the *Angoon*. Our tug groaned, and so did I. We climbed this giant swell about the speed of my dad's '26 Fordson, up, up, and finally we tottered onto the crest.

My stomach flipped and jiggled coffee into my throat as I welded my fingers around a handrail to ride our ship to the bottom of the trough. Another sea mountain rose, and the skipper bounded through the wheelhouse door. We didn't need to report; the next wave was upon us, slightly smaller, but just as wicked. After riding it out, the radio crackled from Adak Station in the Aleutians: Waves as high as 13 stories were wiping out Alaska villages and harbor towns.

After the tail of the tsunami rolled beneath our tug, the skipper suddenly spread out his charts and studied them.

"Get Adak on the line!" he told the bosun. "S***, boys, that d*** wave is headed south — for the Hawaiian Islands!"

We warned Adak Station and figured they'd contact Honolulu — but they never did. Without any warning, the April Fool's Day tsunami struck Hawaii with 45-foot waves and killed 159 people.

৵৵৵

For a Merchant Mariner, it's easy to change ships, but the hardest thing on earth is to walk the gangplank with his sea bag for the last time.

Elaine had never left my heart, and with so many close shaves with death, I pondered over weighing anchor in some peaceful harbor. One day, as I strode the deck of a tug with a cup of coffee, I felt like Jesus sent me a message through nature telling me to settle down. The robins sang sweetly; gulls soared above Anchorage, looking for springtime nesting sites.

I was 23 years old, and I had never really stopped

courting Elaine. I saw her as often as we docked at Seattle and failed miserably at convincing the girl how novel it would be to marry a man of the sea.

The Cook Inlet was as smooth as glass when I said, "Oh, h***."

I threw my coffee cup into the Port of Anchorage, packed my sea bag and walked the plank. I was a full-blown engineer now, a master mechanic for diesel-generated steam systems aboard ships. I could tear 'em down and slap 'em back together blindfolded, so I landed a good job with the City of Anchorage maintaining its power plants.

I radioed Seattle to Elaine (no telephone connections in 1947) that I was a landlubber now and gainfully employed. Would she marry me? Then I let the bait just drift for a few days …

It was her turn to be hooked. One day a whole pile of folks told me to get down to the Alaska Communications office — I had a telegram waiting. They must have read my mail, because they seemed as excited as me.

The telegram had one word typed on the whole page: "Yes."

I call my four years married to Elaine *refreshing*, like tropical ocean spray on the cheeks. But cooling sea mists last but a moment …

Elaine died of a kidney disease, and the same Jesus who had rescued me on the high seas helped me with the hard climb out of darkness once again.

After a heart-wrenching memorial service, I continued to grieve my loss but a short time (except quietly in my soul). Now I had two daughters and an adopted son to raise by myself, and I found God's solace in worshiping at Grandmother Curry's Methodist church. I took the kids with me, and we heard Bible principles taught every Sunday that I wasn't out of town repairing some diesel power plant.

I seldom spoke of my sailing days, and during these family years, my memories anchored in harbors, silent, except in my mind. I understood God's mercy in greater measure and hoped to somehow fulfill my destiny.

I threw myself into being a good father — but my only mentors were ironfisted engineers and my dad. None had stroked me with praise for jobs well done. And in my father's case, it was *his* way or the open sea. I chose the sea.

Now I stood in my father's big boots and with a family, too. How could I possibly balance laundry, school, church, suppertimes and my demanding work? I really needed a good woman, like Elaine, but in *those* perilous waters I felt like I drifted on a life raft again, nudged by hungry sharks.

In decades to come, my family faced monstrous swells every bit as challenging as when Uncle Jim sailed 'round the Horn of Africa — and God only knows how we survived it.

తతత

It was 20 below zero the day I smelled rotten onions at Kenai's natural gas booster plant. I had arrived by helicopter from Anchorage to troubleshoot why the engines stopped cold. Leaning over a turbine, I mentioned the stink to one of the three gas plant technicians.

He brushed me off, and suddenly *I was somewhere else.*

I lay in a snow bank, sizzling. I beat my herringbone coveralls, trying to put out flames, then I realized my hair was burning. I burrowed headfirst into the snow, scooping a man-sized hole as fast as my burned hands would let me. After a few seconds of cooling my torso, I rolled out, dazed and trying to piece together why I sat in a cold snowdrift.

Wasn't I just standing indoors beside a turbine?

A man hollered from somewhere.

"Eldon!" One of the natural gas workers, arms peeling and burned, stumbled up. "Go shut down the equalizing valve. Hurry! We've got more than 900 pounds of pressurized gas ready to blow if some spark gets to it."

I suffered from shock and barely noticed the skin on my fingers and palms sticking to the cold iron wheel after I yanked my hands away. The valve was off, and the plant was safe now, so I joined the three technicians standing in shocked silence. None of the vehicles in the lot had any window glass anymore. Some were missing doors. Shelves inside one van had been blown through the front like shrapnel. We found one truck operable and crowded inside.

George, the foreman of the plant, climbed behind the wheel, but something told me he wasn't quite all there.

"Gotta get to the Rainbow Bar! Gotta get to the Rainbow Bar, in Kenai! Ya know? Gotta get …"

Thank God for the high snow berms on the auxiliary road, or we never would have made it to the highway. We bounced between the berms like a pinball, and George never glanced in either direction as he swept into the long curve toward his Rainbow Bar. An ambulance came into view, sirens wailing, and the paramedics noticed us — I guess the missing windshield gave us away.

But shell-shocked George never paused. He had a date with a barstool. I grabbed the keys out of the ignition and tossed them out the big hole where the windshield should have been.

I spent a week in the hospital, hairless and bandaged up like a mummy. Something strange happened to me about that time as I ruminated on my brush with death. I had been blown completely outdoors, along with the walls of the natural gas plant, yet I survived. Deep in my heart God confirmed that my life was not my own. I belonged to the one who'd saved me one more time.

By the time a man is 79 years old, he pretty well knows what he's looking for in a woman. Fine lines have their place, but it's what powers the lovely vessel that holds a man steady to his purpose and on a peaceful course.

THE FATE OF THE MARINER

I had settled in Wasilla, where I lived alone in a house my grandson and I built from stem to stern. I arrived at my homeport for some R and R after a three-month stretch on Shemya Island in the Aleutian Chain, where I supervised an overhaul of an Air Force power plant.

My daughter invited me to attend a little church called Sunny Knik Chapel — and the first time I visited, a feeling akin to a seaman's weather sense kicked in. I just *knew* I should join up with this loyal crew.

As I worshipped God at Sunny Knik, I heard the voice of Jesus, crystal clear in a way I had never known, and within months, I was destined to find the woman I had waited decades to find.

Her name is Rose.

When I stopped for a bite to eat at the Houston (Alaska) senior center, I noticed this young woman in the galley. (Later I found out that she was watching me, too.) A voice in my heart told me that this beautiful Rose was good.

I hadn't dated in more than 20 years, and Rose was a professional woman from Brooklyn, 10 years my junior. For much of her life she had assisted in operating rooms at a busy New York hospital. We were both entering uncharted waters, and I battened down the hatches before asking her out.

I forgot my wallet on our first outing, and guess who paid for dinner? I figured that I had spoiled my chances for another date — but that's what I love about my Rose. She has never jumped ship in the midst of a squall.

Lucky for me.

Over the next few months, we fell head over heels in love, and Rose felt the same about the Sunny Knik Chapel as I did. She felt God speak to her there, too. Both of us abandoned our stuffy, liturgical past to follow Jesus, who I believe cares more about our hearts than about spit-polished shoes.

Neither of us ever thought we would marry again, but that was before we met.

I told her, "Honey, ya' know, I think we better go see the preacher."

"You mean it, Eldon?" she said.

Wow, was I relieved.

How God matched me with *exactly* the right mate after all these lonely years is more than a blessing — it's a miracle. Rose says that she came to Alaska and found the face of God — in wonderful friends, in her worship of Jesus and in the majesty of the Last Frontier.

I see God's reflection, too — in my Rosemary.

My purpose for living has never been clearer: I offer my life as a chart for others to study and sail by. Every wrinkle and scar tells the story of God's mercy toward a seaman who sails for the Master Mariner of eternal seas.

THE FATE OF THE MARINER

My Home Town
By Tom: Poet of the Long Time Tommy

A lot of men who sail on ships come from some small town,
Far away from harbors where there are no ships around.
And that's the only place they know, until they go to sea,
Until they go they swear that it's the only place to be.

Before I left my home I used to watch the moon up there,
And I'd swear those hometown moonbeams were the best of
anywhere.
I sang about our sunsets, the bees and the birds,
With starry-eyed expression and a lot of fancy words.

The hometown grass was greener, no sky was quite so blue,
The water in the lakes was even wetter, too.
The flowers there were sweeter and I'd say with a dreamy face,
That mother nature had never been to any other place.

But as I grew I longed for the world I'd never seen,
And the blue horizon whispered, "Come on, you're 17."
So one day I left and I've been sailing lots of years,
Over lots of oceans, and a couple of hemispheres.

And one thing that I've learned is that the sun can warm your heart,
From Boston to Calcutta; Missouri to Momart.
For I've seen a flaming sun that splashed the Texas skies,
And across the world I've seen it do the same above Shanghai.

I have sailed out of Frisco and looked up at the moon,
And watched it sail beside me cross the ocean to Rangoon.
And another thing I've learned is that those moonbeams I saw,
Were the same ones that shine on the corner grocery store.

PERILOUS TIDES

And if you sail around the world, no matter where you are,
Looking up from the deck of the ship, you'd see your hometown star.
Winking at lovers as far off as Paree (or some kid in China),
Who scribes "I love you" on a tree.

So now when I see the hills or trees, I always get impressed,
I never get to thinking where or which is best.
For I've walked the hills of Oregon and listened to the trees,
And they sound the same in Swedish, or Dutch, or Portuguese.

And now when I hear a robin sing it sounds just as sweet,
In Cape Town or Palermo or the island of Papeete.
And when I pick a rose beside the Zuider Zee,
It smells just like a rose the girl in Brooklyn gave to me.

So if everyone thinks his hometown is the best hometown there is,
I guess that's right; it is the best! Yours, and mine, and his!
For every place is best and you learn the truth of that,
When you get to see the beauty — wherever you hang your hat.

THE LOGGING TRAIL
The Story of Eric
Written by Marty Minchin

I muttered to myself as I opened the heavy screen door, my words dripping with preteen attitude. Another day, another fight with my mom before I even left the house for school.

"Eric," she called sternly. I turned to face her.

The springs were broken in the door's hinges, and Mom had stopped it before it closed. Quick as a striking snake, she raised her hand to flat palm me across the face.

I'd seen this move a thousand times before, and this time I was ready. Like an action star in a slow-motion film sequence, I grabbed her wrist with one hand and pushed her arm away from my face mid-slap. Her eyes widened; I'd never fought back before.

But Mom wasn't done. While I momentarily reveled in the successful retaliation I'd planned in my mind for years, she slammed the butt of her other palm under my cheekbone and shot me a triumphant look as I stumbled back. I bowed my chest and stepped toward her threateningly, but then thought twice, turned and slunk off after my friend Leo toward the bus stop. The overcast day in Southern California reflected my perpetually angry mood.

"What happened to your face, man?" a kid questioned me at the bus stop. The red mark on my cheek was already turning into a bruise. I marched out my usual excuse and blamed the bully down the street who weighed 100 pounds more than me and regularly tried to beat me up.

"Ralph did it." I looked down to cover up my lie.

"No, he didn't," Leo said, laughing. "It was his mom."

For the first time in my life, I fessed up. "Yeah, my mom hit me," I said quietly.

And for the last time in my life, my mom had hit me. I wasn't that big at age 12, but I was finally big enough to stand up to her. But the anger and curse words that she had rained down on me for 12 years remained with me. Some moms transfer love to their children with hugs and kisses. My mom hammered in her legacy with punches and slaps.

❧ ❧ ❧

My mom began abusing me before I can remember. Born the middle child between two daughters, I became the sole target of her wrath. She beat me with her hand, the rod from the Venetian blinds and sticks she snapped off trees in the front yard. She'd whip the leather belt out of my pants and spank me with it.

One time she kicked a screen door open on me and sprained a few of my fingers. I'd curl up in a corner while she beat whatever part of me she could reach. When my older sister was 7 and I was 2, she filled a little bag with some necessities and tried to run away with me to get me away from Mom.

My mom was a stout woman of medium height, with dark hair and eyes and a voice that seemed to be permanently yelling. She never nurtured, and the fire of her anger burned just beneath her skin, ready to burst out at the slightest offense.

Nighttimes posed a problem for me. Mom slept lightly, and I had a small bladder. I wet my bed until I was 8 or 9 years old, and when I finally began waking up at night to urinate, the moment the liquid hit the toilet water, Mom would stir and seconds later scream at me to be quiet. In our small one-bathroom house, my options for nighttime relief were limited. To avoid her wrath, I eventually began using the corner of my room.

Dad would sometimes fall victim to my mom's abuse. A soft-spoken man who had served a tour in Vietnam that he rarely talked about, he was two-thirds of my mom's size. She reveled in degrading him in front of us, criticizing him for everything from chewing his food too loudly to biting his fingernails. He rarely cursed or even talked, for that matter. Instead of asking us directly how our days were, he'd ask Mom. He avoided conflict at all cost.

I still don't understand why Mom targeted me. My best explanation is that my older sister has another dad, and maybe Mom loved her differently because she raised her for two years as a single mom. My younger sister was a miracle child, born after my parents weren't expecting to have any more children. She was their precious baby.

❧ ❧ ❧

Mom was a bully until someone challenged her, and otherwise she was a follower. She and my dad felt passionately about nothing, and when my mom's sister led them into the Mormon church, my parents trailed right along. I was 18 months old when they joined.

Surprisingly, my parents became devout Mormons — on the outside. We faithfully attended temple services and the congregation's many family activities, such as picnics and camping, that were designed to keep members close together and close to the church. Straying from the church's strict moral teachings, I learned, had humiliating consequences.

My chauvinist stepgrandfather practically handed me my first major temptation, long before I was baptized into the Mormon church at age 8. My cousins and I regularly visited his house, often flipping through his stash of *Playboy* magazines. I knew I wasn't supposed to be looking at pictures of naked women, but I was curious. After running around outside, climbing trees and playing tag, it was all too easy to settle onto the couch and leaf through a magazine. We knew where to find his stash, which he rarely bothered to hide.

My punishment came in the Mormon Sunday church services.

Anytime I advanced in my religious instruction in church, I had to meet with the bishop, who was our pastor. These meetings, which came regularly when I was around 12, 14 and 16 and on my birthdays, involved the bishop sitting behind his desk and interviewing me. If I admitted to any sins, Mormons believed he had the authority to forgive and punish me.

I had plenty to confess. Depending on my age, I told the bishop about looking at pornography, heavy petting with girls or masturbation. He then doled out my sentence and made sure that everyone in the church knew about it.

Sunday services were the worst. Every week, we'd eat a small piece of bread and drink a tiny cup of water to remember the story of Jesus dying on the cross. Adolescent and teenage boys, dressed in white shirts and ties on their way to becoming priests themselves in the church, passed plates holding the bread and cups down the pews.

If the bishop had deemed me unworthy, which he usually did for at least six months, I had to pass the plate to the person next to me without taking bread or water for myself. I'd shamefully hand the plate to my seatmate and stare down at my empty hands. They might pretend not to look, but everyone around me knew I'd had to pass.

Despite the regular humiliation, I stayed outwardly faithful to the church. I regularly attended Saturday night dances, where Mormon teenagers were encouraged to make friends and look for future mates. I mostly enjoyed all of the girls there. I spent the early mornings of my high school years in seminary, pre-dawn classes for students about the Bible and Mormon teachings. All I remember learning was that I could never be as perfect as I was supposed to be. And I became extremely judgmental of everyone else who couldn't achieve those same standards.

≈≈≈

I was plotting my life out long before I finished high school. My parents had always struggled financially, and I'd grown up in a cramped house 20 miles east of Los Angeles. By the time I graduated, I'd already bailed my parents out of near-foreclosure twice with money I earned from part-time jobs.

My goals were to make a lot of money, buy a house and look good doing it. My friend Travis and I secured a mortgage together when I was 19, reasoning that by going in together we could afford a bigger place. I drove a forest green Volkswagen Jetta lowered on 15-inch chrome rims. My job as a car stereo installation manager at Circuit City paid well, and I made sure that my car had the biggest, loudest stereo possible. When I rolled up to a stoplight, the cars around me vibrated along with my booming bass.

Even more than having nice things, I loved showing them off. My friends and I spent many afternoons playing basketball at the park accompanied by my car stereo, which I turned on full blast. I'd whip out my Visa Gold card, reveling in its flashy metallic finish, when my friends and I went to dinner. At the bars, I cavalierly told my friends to just pay their cover charge; I'd pick up the drinks. I did make decent money, but not as much as I acted like I did.

My childhood exposure to porn had grown along with me, and now I'd tag along with buddies to strip joints, feigning disinterest but secretly feeling thrilled. I'd occasionally buy a magazine, and when porn sites began popping up on the Internet, I'd sometimes take a look. I loved girls in real life even more than the ones in the magazines, and I quickly learned that telling a girl what she wanted to hear could get me what I wanted.

My high school years were filled with baseball and wrestling teams and part-time work. When a buddy introduced me to weed, I liked it and smoked the infrequent joint. That turned into every weekend and then every day on my lunch break.

When my friend Ray suggested at a party that I try something harder, it was an easy yes. We'd already had plenty to drink, and the answer flowed smoothly out of me.

Ray pulled out a light bulb, dropped the crystal of speed into the upside-down bulb and heated it up with a lighter. I breathed in the smoke deeply, as the faraway voice of my conscience reminded me that I'd taken a big step toward more involved use.

As long as I'm not snorting anything, I'm not a druggy, I argued back.

Ray and I spent the weekend together, and it didn't take me long to realize that the high from snorting speed was significantly more powerful than breathing smoke from a light bulb pipe.

An addiction needs to be fed to avoid the plunging

crash from coming off a high, and for several months, I channeled much of my Circuit City paycheck into my drug habit. When I was fired from Circuit City for fighting with a guy on the job, I was hired at Good Guys and soon met a customer who gave me a rock of cocaine.

The truth was, as great as the coke made me feel, I realized my life was terrible. It was a matter of time before I got busted at work, and thankfully I had not been pulled over — yet — while driving impaired. My rehabilitation program? Enlisting in the Navy. By then, I'd been fired from Good Guys for trying to give a customer an unauthorized discount, and I was losing my house with Travis.

In the meantime, I got a job with UPS and moved back in with my mom, who had divorced my dad after 23 years of marriage.

As a retail manager, I had seen plenty of job applications that asked whether you had served in the military, and if you had, whether you were honorably or dishonorably discharged. I knew that if I ever had to check "dishonorably" on a job application, my chances of getting hired anywhere were nil.

I had nine months to get clean, and I cut back on the drugs and reduced my imbibing to alcohol and an infrequent joint.

On the other hand, I had no reason to cut back on the girls. I liked gorgeous women, the ones everyone wanted. My first-choice girl was Eileen, an exotic half-Japanese, half-Hispanic beauty who had been a year behind me in high school. She and I had an on-and-off relationship, and we were off when I enlisted. But before I left for boot camp, I decided I wanted her back.

Laura, my current girlfriend, was the only obstacle. When I called Eileen to test the waters for a reconciliation, she balked at the mention of Laura. As soon as I hung up the phone, I dialed Laura's number.

"It's over," I told my shocked girlfriend. "I'm looking forward to the future, and you're not someone I see myself with."

I waited less than 24 hours to call Eileen to report my newly single status, and within hours we were back together.

As the date approached for me to leave for boot camp, our relationship became more serious. I overlooked some glaring issues to keep her as a trophy on my arm. Lots of guys wanted to date her, and I liked that she had chosen to be with me. But she didn't like my outgoing personality and was embarrassed by my jokes, so much so that I became two different people. With her, I was reserved and reined in my humor to keep the peace and save an argument. When she wasn't around, I could be the life of the party.

Before I shipped out, I committed to Eileen — who I had now been with on and off for almost five years — in my heart. I knew she would wait for me.

❧❧❧

I was tired of feeling like a loser inside, so I wanted to make joining the Navy extraordinary by training for the Special Forces and trying out for the Navy Seals.

I was still drinking and smoking weed a little, but I pumped up my workout schedule to early morning sessions of running, swimming and pushups. I spent nine months getting into the best shape I'd ever been in. Travis, my best friend and fellow partier, was a great encourager during that time. If I had been up late drinking and tried to sleep in, he'd make sure to wake me up. A month before I left for Basic Training, where I'd take the test for the Navy Seals, I gave up the habits that could taint my impending drug test.

While at boot camp in Great Lakes, Illinois, I had the opportunity to work out and train with other Navy Seals who were waiting to be transferred. Six weeks into it, the Navy doctor called me into her office.

The doctor got right to the point. "You can't be a Seal," she told me. I stared at her in disbelief.

"Your eyesight is too bad."

I knew my eyesight wasn't perfect, but it had never been an issue before.

"It's correctable," I said, confident that she had overlooked that aspect of my vision.

She pulled out the literature about eyesight requirements in the Navy, rifling through the papers.

"These are the parameters." She pointed out the numbers on the page. "I can't do anything about it. We have to drop you from the program."

The disappointment crashed down so hard that I started to cry. The doctor tried to offer some condolence.

"You can still be a Navy diver," she said.

"Navy divers are a bunch of wusses," I muttered. I was done with the Special Forces and instead took a job as a Navy firefighter.

My new job on a ship took me all over the world and away from Eileen. I hit the town in Mexico with a buddy during two days of leave, and after getting tanked, I spent a wild night with his sister-in-law. When my ship stopped in Australia, only three weeks before I was scheduled to see Eileen after a six-month deployment, I spent the night with a woman I met there. I was actually surprised that those were the only times I'd cheated during that trip.

The phone had worked for me before, so I used it to break the news to Eileen when she was away visiting friends in California. I got drunk watching a Lakers basketball game with some friends and dialed her number. My slurred speech was all it took for her to get mad, so I just suggested she'd also probably want to stay in California, anyway, after she heard what I'd done.

Surprisingly, she came back, and we spent eight months in relationship counseling. She hated the Mormon church, which wanted us to go to a Mormon counselor, so I let her choose the counselor. Anytime my life hit the toilet, I headed back to the Mormons in hopes of straightening myself out. My nights were filled with Alcoholics Anonymous meetings and counseling, and all that came of it was a mutual realization that Eileen and I shouldn't be together. My heart, though, had already left Eileen. My emotional break came one night after a strange dream.

In relationship counseling, we had been talking about how I needed to ask for forgiveness from Eileen. She was struggling to forgive me. In my dream, that issue was manifested in a knock on the door.

I answered it. Before me stood a figure that I recognized immediately. His features matched the painting of Jesus that hung prominently in my family's Mormon church. His brown hair parted cleanly in the middle and reached his shoulders, framing a strong, serious face. His mustache and beard were recently trimmed, giving him the look of a hip 1970s businessman.

My mind moved to a story I remembered from the Bible. Jesus had just eaten a meal with some of his closest followers when he offered to wash their feet. The followers were horrified because foot washing was below someone of Jesus' status as a religious teacher. Jesus rebuffed them and washed their feet, anyway, telling them that the best way to be a leader was to be a servant.

In my dream, I invited Jesus in, and he sat down on the couch as I pulled a basin from the kitchen cupboard. I filled it with water and sat at his feet, washing them in the cool water from the sink.

I looked at his serene face, and the words that were crying out in my heart wouldn't come out of my mouth.

Forgive me, Jesus. Forgive me again.

He heard my silent plea, and with a gentle gesture, laid

his hands on my head. I grabbed his wrists and cried out with the realization that Jesus had forgiven me.

My real cry startled me awake, and I shook Eileen.

"Guess what just happened to me!" I was bursting to tell her about the real feeling of forgiveness I'd sensed. I described the dream.

"What does that mean?" She looked skeptical.

"I've been forgiven."

Eileen wasn't convinced, and she lay quiet for a moment.

"How could God forgive you before I forgive you?"

It all went downhill with Eileen from there. But something real had been sparked between God and me.

☙☙☙☙

My next assignment in the Navy was serving as a fire chief on a ship. I was always on the lookout for girls, and Chelsea, with brown hair and eyes, was the best-looking woman on the boat. She was fun, and my friends liked her. She didn't drink herself, but she didn't make an issue of it when I did. And when I joked around, she laughed. Chelsea worked under me as an assistant fire chief, and I enjoyed hanging out with her in the ship's gym and with our ship friends. There was a light inside her that I couldn't identify, but I sensed that she was different.

Physically, though, she wasn't my typical type. It was months before her beauty caught my attention in a new way.

When Chelsea needed a ride to Oregon that Christmas, I offered to take her. I thought she was cool, and I wouldn't mind spending a few hours on the road getting to know her. My plan was to drop her off at her family's house and head to Las Vegas to spend my Christmas holiday partying with friends. Chelsea's father, a pastor, would drive her back to the ship after Christmas.

We made good time and pulled up to her family's logging property early on December 24. The family had owned this land along a logging road for nearly 100 years, and the tall trees and quiet sounds of nature captivated me. The bars indicating a signal on my cell phone all but disappeared the closer we got to Chelsea's grandfather's house.

I had the whole day to spend there, so I followed Chelsea around as she introduced me to her grandparents and numerous aunts, uncles and cousins. We headed across the road to visit Siri, her cousin and close friend, that afternoon. Her uncle Jim opened the door, his wide smile welcoming us in before he even said hello.

We got to talking, and Jim and I had a lot in common. A retired Navy man himself, he understood me better than I realized.

"What are you doing for Christmas?" he asked. I wasn't about to tell Chelsea's uncle that I was headed out for a weekend of boozing.

"Um, I'm going back to the ship to spend time with some friends."

He slapped me on the back.

"No, you're not. You're going to go back and get drunk."

Was this man psychic?

"No, I'm not."

Jim knew the truth. "You're staying here."

"I don't even know you guys," I protested weakly.

"You're staying here."

I stayed. And my life was changed.

❧❧❧

Jim and his wife, Ella, gave me their sons' room for the night. It still had the original Captain America carpet and sports team memorabilia on the shelves, even though their boys had long ago grown up and moved out. I marveled at my awkward but strangely comfortable day where a tight-knit family had welcomed a stranger for the holidays.

The family gathered again early Christmas morning, the cousins spilling over the couches and chairs as the large clan filled the room. Not knowing where or how I fit in, I excused myself to drive down the hill, where I hoped there was a strong enough cell signal to call my family and wish them Merry Christmas.

I returned to find a place for me in the circle of relatives. Under my seat was a stack of gifts, each with a nametag:

To: Eric, From: Santa

To: Eric, From: Rudolph

To: Eric, From: The Wise Men

Following family tradition, each cousin opened a gift in turn around the circle. There were enough gifts under my seat so that each time the turn came to me, I had something to unwrap.

Each gift held money, a combination of bills and coins. I ended the morning with $27.60. It was a small amount compared to the money I had earned at other times in my life, but the total represented something far more valuable: love and acceptance from a family full of love for each other and for God.

Those people didn't know me from Adam. I slept in their house and opened gifts with their children, a surreal experience of feeling like I was part of a family when I was away from my family. My birth family was a picture-perfect Mormon family on Sundays and a jacked-up mess once the house door closed. Jim and Ella and Chelsea's bevy of cousins and relatives were the real deal, genuine inside and out. I still didn't know God personally, but that day somewhere inside me, I learned more about the real character of Jesus than I had in years of faithful attendance at the Mormon church.

დოდოდო

Chelsea and I began to date after that Christmas. She loved God and had a relationship with him that she was trying to restore. She led the worship singing at the ship's Christian Sunday service, which I attended mostly because I wanted to make sure the other guys weren't hitting on her. I was still tangling with the bishop at my Mormon church, trying to work through my many sins and get out of trouble with the church.

I met with the bishop a final time in the summer of 2000, just before Chelsea and I planned to travel to Alaska where her parents lived. The bishop forbade me to make the trip, as it meant I would miss a few Sunday services. I reminded him that I was an adult, and I didn't need another adult telling me what to do.

The bishop was ready for me when I got back home and faced my disciplinary hearing for defying his orders. He sat across his desk and glared at me as other leaders in the church took notes on our conversation.

I told the bishop about my trip and about the physical relationship that Chelsea and I had at times, which the church regarded as inappropriate for an unmarried couple. Then I walked into the church foyer to await my sentence.

There hung a portrait of Jesus, the popular Mormon depiction of him that had starred in my dream. It was the only face of Jesus I had ever known. I sat down and looked at him.

I need to be done with this church, I told him. *If I need to be punished, okay. Just let me start again from scratch. Forgive me.*

The bishop's sharp voice called me back into his office for the verdict.

"Brother Eric," he intoned. "What do you think we should do with you?"

Clearly, we were all fed up with my regular offenses.

"I request to be ex-communicated from the Mormon church."

The bishop's eyes widened into saucers. He blinked repeatedly as he absorbed my announcement, then adjusted his tactics.

"We prayed," he began slowly, "and … we agree."

There. It was done, once and for all.

"Thank you very much." I stood up, nodded a goodbye to two decades of fruitless religion and stepped out of the church into the sunshine of Everett, Washington. Whether it was truly sunny that day, or if it only felt sunny due to my newly lifted burdens, I'll never know. The invisible bonds and chains of guilt that had tied me to the Mormon religion fell off at the door and were swallowed into the dark building as I strode away.

Was there ever a more peaceful day? Not yet in my lifetime.

ॐॐॐ

Chelsea and I knew we were going to get married. During a particularly rough time in our relationship, her dad had even told her not to give up on me. I had always planned to fly to Alaska and ask her dad properly for her hand in marriage, even though I also planned to marry Chelsea regardless of his answer. My plans didn't change when we found out she was pregnant.

We flew to Alaska, and I met her dad at his night job

as a security officer at a car dealership in Wasilla. We sat in the cab of his truck in the cold and the dark, the engine humming to keep the heater going.

I asked for her hand in marriage. He wasn't surprised.

"We knew this was coming, and her mom and I have been talking," he began. "We could see where this relationship was going. You have our blessing." I basked in the warmth of his acceptance, knowing it could end in the next breath.

"There's one more thing," I began, slowing my words to delay the bad news. "Chelsea's with child."

I glanced at Chelsea's dad, who looked like I had punched him in the gut.

"But I want you to know that's not why I'm asking you if I can marry her," I hurriedly added. "That's why I'm doing it now. I just had to move everything forward."

He was concerned that we get married right away. He wanted to know how we would raise the child.

I knew I didn't want my children to grow up in California. The beauty and simplicity of Alaska had touched me deeply already, and I knew this was a better place for a family. In California, people lived like they had money to spare when they usually didn't. In Alaska, people with money to spare lived so modestly you'd never know they made six figures. People in Alaska weren't aware of my history. If I could get away from my old friends and my old life, I might have a chance of staying on track.

Chelsea and I married in June and moved to Wasilla.

While the move and marriage had gotten me away from many bad influences, some of those impulses stayed with me. I still looked at porn sometimes. I drank after work. We were barely making ends meet. We were comfortable, but not really happy.

We attended Chelsea's family's church, Sunny Knik Chapel, and soon I found myself leading the church's youth group. I wasn't a Bible scholar, but I could speak articulately about learning from hard life experiences. My passionate entreaties for teenagers to change their lives covered up my own lack of spiritual knowledge. I got baptized in April of 2002 because I thought it was the right thing to do. That led to a phone fight with my mom, who told me that if I wasn't Mormon I wasn't anything to God and getting baptized in what she referred to as "their church" meant nothing. I reminded her that this was not "their church" — it was God's church. While Mom was still staunchly Mormon, we were still able to talk. In the times I've tried to discuss my faith with my dad, he has seemed more open to listening. I'm so thankful for the new relationship I've built with him now that I'm an adult and can see him for the caring, interesting man he is.

Halloween of 2004 fell on a Sunday, which is why I never forget the date. The worship team began singing a song during the church service that day that prompted me to think about my own relationship with God. Had I ever fully committed my life to following God? Did I trust my life and my future to him? Did I really have a relationship with him where I was getting to know God better?

The answer was clear: No.

I had to tell everyone, even though the Sunday service was in full swing around me.

I stood up at my pew and spoke as soon as the music quieted.

"I'm sorry," I began. The congregation gaped at this unusual admission from an established church leader. "I just wanted you guys to know that I just gave my heart to the Lord. I thought I was saved, but I wasn't. I've been living a lie."

My church acquaintances weren't the only ones in shock. Chelsea and her father stared at me, eyes wide, as well. It had been pretty easy to act like a Christian in front of the church congregation — I'd seen my parents do it for years. Now I needed to get my inner life in order, too.

≈≈≈≈

From then on, things were different, starting with my longtime secret relationship with pornography. I had graduated from *Playboy* to strip clubs to Internet porn, which I still occasionally looked at on my computer. My only weapon against it, before now, had been my own imperfect willpower.

I confessed to Chelsea and a friend, who also had struggled with pornography and who became my accountability partner. If I felt tempted to look, I would call him. We prayed together and asked God to free me from my entanglement with pornography. I stopped going to the gym, where women often dressed in ways that triggered impure thoughts. My problems became less hidden as I talked with Chelsea and my friend, and I found that sharing the burden of my struggles with people who loved me made them easier to carry.

The more I loved God, the more I wanted to please him. One night in 2008, Chelsea and I attended a youth conference closing worship service, and at the end we walked to the front of the room and asked the speaker to pray for me. I wanted those images of women that popped into my mind at the most unexpected times to disappear from my memory. Chelsea grabbed my hand, and the three of us begged for healing and that I would win my battle against pornography.

God responded. Chelsea and I felt ourselves fill up with God's presence that night, a feeling that confirmed to us that God heard us and was responding in a way that we could sense.

"We're done with this," I told Chelsea, my voice full of emotion. "God has given us the victory that we needed."

I haven't looked at pornography since.

৵৵৵

The summer days in Alaska are long, the sunlight stretching long into the nighttime hours. I used these long days to build my growing family — now with two children and a house outside of Wasilla. After working a full day at my job, I'd have a picnic dinner with Chelsea and the kids, who would meet me at the construction site. She'd then take the kids home for bath and bedtime, and I'd work until 2:30 or 3 a.m. because it was still light. We painted the three-bedroom, two-bath house yellow with white trim, and one friend called it "the light on the hill," a description I particularly liked.

Between my job as a superintendent at a heating and air conditioning company and Chelsea's part-time job, we made a pretty decent income. She and I met with a financial advisor about retiring by the time we were 50. We knocked out our debt until we only owed on our mortgage and started building up our savings.

Then, two missionaries spoke at our church.

They had spent years in Kenya, but had left in the 80s at the request of the Kenyan president. In the early 2000s, the country had a new president, and the missionaries could return.

Chelsea and I had toyed with the idea of going on a mission trip. We had discussed working with Mercy Ships, which sails to different countries to provide relief, or doing short-term missions in Paraguay. The night John and Joy spoke at our church, God spoke to my heart, *It's not Mercy Ships or Paraguay. It's Kenya, the Pokok people John and Joy worked with.*

Really, God? I thought. *You've got to be kidding me.*

There's no way I could tell Chelsea that God was telling me we should move to Kenya. I kept it from her for two weeks, wondering how I would ever broach the subject with her, even though my sense that God wanted us in Africa was only growing stronger. What was I supposed to say? "Let's sell our house that I built and give up that money and go live in the bush in Africa?"

Instead, I prayed that God would deliver the same message to Chelsea.

She called my cell phone one day while I was driving between jobs.

"Can you talk?" she asked. "What did you think of John and Joy's presentation?"

"You go first," I told her anxiously.

"I don't think we're supposed to go with Mercy Ships. Paraguay, either."

I was dumbfounded, and the only thing I could get out was, "Yep."

Then, my confession flowed out. "I've been praying for two weeks that God would make you say something!" I told her. The conversation was easy from there. What would our lives' legacy be? What did we want to teach our children about priorities and living a life that reflected our relationships with God?

❧ ❧ ❧

The Wasilla Craigslist classified ads were soon filled with our postings. We sold our snow machines and the boat. We got rid of canoes and catamarans, leather furniture and even our house, everything our hard work had earned.

We were left with a few sentimental keepsakes, the

clothes on our backs and plane tickets to Kenya. We moved into my in-laws' modest house.

Between 2011 and 2012, we spent about a year in Kenya working with the Pokok people and in a nearby city. I met with pastors and other men who lived in areas so rural there was no electricity or running water, and all four of us worked with missionaries in a nearby city who were establishing a home for young girls who escaped the sex trade. We brought people food, counseled them and became their friends. We learned that when you show people love, it can bring about amazing change, regardless of whether you're with them for a day or a year.

After two trips to Kenya, we returned to Wasilla to pray about our next steps. With no debt, few possessions and a willingness to follow God's promptings, we were open and available for anything. In return, amazing and unexpected things have happened.

Chelsea and I were offered our jobs back, although neither of us asked. In January, I'll own the company where I'd worked so long. We're willing to go back to Kenya, if we sense God telling us to. If not, for now, we're in a financial position to help pay for others who do go.

First thing every morning, before the kids wake up and the sun is shining too brightly, Chelsea and I head downstairs to start our day. These days, that place could be her parents' house or a friend's place where we've been housesitting. Soon it will be on the deck of the 570-square-foot apartment I'm building for us over a two-car garage in her parents' yard.

Money, I've learned, is better used in God's hands than mine. We've downsized.

I turn on the coffee machine and sit down in the Lazy Boy. By the time the coffee is brewed, Chelsea has settled into a chair near me, and we quietly read our own Bibles to ourselves. I've learned that talking to God and reading the Bible before I eat breakfast starts the day on the right foot.

In my mind on these mornings, I often walk the logging trails on Grandpa's property in Oregon.

I've hiked those trails for years when we've visited Chelsea's family, often by myself, carrying a cup of coffee. No matter what time of year, the trail is peaceful, and the air is cool and crisp on my face. A slight mist usually falls over the path, carrying the scent of cedar and evergreens. Sometimes deer and elk wander by. It was here that God brought me peace and a new family who showed me what it's like to love God and love each other.

Chelsea never looks more beautiful to me than when she reads her Bible and prays on these quiet mornings downstairs. It's hard not to steal glances at her, the morning light shining on her still figure, and smile.

A VERITABLE JOY
The Story of Sue Ann
Written by Laura L. Florio

"No! You can't take her! Please don't take my baby," I sobbed. Little DeeDee held a firm grasp on my blouse, and her sweet pale face turned red and contorted with wailing. Barely old enough to understand what was happening, she was beyond consolation of any sort.

It was a scene of utter chaos. The officers assigned to the case were in tears as were my 4-year-old daughter, my ex-husband, Evan, and I. Only Evan's new wife, Natalie, stood silently and triumphantly, her lips pursed tightly together, her hands clenched at her sides.

The policeman gently but firmly untangled DeeDee's hands and did his best to keep her from wriggling free as he placed her in her father's arms.

"Mama!" Her young voice ripped through my heart, and I turned away and crumpled to the floor in pure unadulterated despair. The footsteps faded, but the weeping continued, even as DeeDee, her father and Natalie exited the room.

"Ma'am, I'm afraid you're going to have to come with me." The officer laid his hand on my back and helped me to my feet. Slowly, he turned me toward the door and, with the escort of the female officer, directed me through the long corridor to an empty cell known as the drunk tank. *And I'm not even drunk,* I thought.

The officer led me to a bench, and I collapsed as a wave of grief overcame me. As he closed the door, he said with watery eyes, "Ma'am, if there is anything, I mean anything, I can do for you, just let me know. I regret I was the S.O.B. who had to arrest you."

❧ ❧ ❧

Though only supposed to be held in temporary custody until Evan, Natalie and DeeDee made it safely home, I remained in jail for five days. During that time I wept unceasingly until the corners of my eyes bled from rawness. Despite the kindness of the officers, who went to great measures to make my stay as comfortable and dignified as possible, I saw nothing but my own veil of tears. Eating was utterly unthinkable. Sleeping came only in fits, and I always awoke crying.

When they finally released me, they sent me directly to Dallas, Oregon, to face contempt of court charges. The judge sentenced me to six months of probation and supervised visitation at Evan and Natalie's house every other week. It proved to be a hellish sentence. For the next seven years, Natalie often met me at the door with an excuse as to why DeeDee wasn't available to see me. "DeeDee is being punished," she would say. Then she'd turn on her heel and slam the door shut.

In those moments, the hatred boiled up inside of me so intensely, it required all my self-control not to attack her. Instead, I only smiled. I knew if my actions did not belie my feelings, I would risk losing all visitations with DeeDee. "Kill her with kindness" became my motto. That, and I hired as many lawyers as possible to try to win back custody. Finally, I pleaded enough with a judge to allow the visitations to take place at my parents' home. This improved the situation slightly for me, but not for DeeDee. One evening, I convinced Evan to let me take her to see the movie *Cinderella*. Throughout the entire movie, she cried and whimpered, "It's just like at my house." Natalie had two daughters.

◈◈◈

"Do you take this man to be your lawfully wedded husband?"

The air was ripe with pause, and I felt my future hang in the balance. I gazed into Evan's eyes. They were both kind and committed — in a proud, dutiful sort of way. There was love there, I thought, but this couldn't possibly end well. He's my friend, not the tall, dark and handsome man I dreamed of marrying. Yet here I was, pregnant and 18. Marriage was unavoidable at this stage. I drew in a long breath. "I do."

"To have and to hold from this day forward, to love and to cherish in sickness and in health?"

"I do." The ceremony dragged on, my answers curt and calculated. I recalled the drive to Boise, Idaho, where my aunt lived, and the phone conversations we both had to have with our parents.

"You have to call your parents first," my aunt stated firmly. "I'll not have my relatives coming to my house with a shotgun because I allowed their children to get hitched without permission."

"Oh, Barb," I said, giggling. "That would never happen."

My aunt suppressed a smile and nodded toward the phone. "Make the call."

I dialed the number to my parents in Dallas, Oregon. "Mom?" My voice shook a little.

"Yes?"

"I'm at Aunt Barb's house … with Evan. We're getting married — that is — if we have your permission."

There was a pause, and I sensed my mother recalibrating her composure. "This is a little sudden, Sue Ann, but of course, you know we think of Evan as one of the family. Your father and I are pleased."

"Thanks, Mom." I breathed a sigh of relief. "I have to go. Evan has to call his parents."

"Okay, give my best to Barb. Have a good wedding and Happy New Year."

"Thanks." The line clicked, and I handed the phone to Evan.

"Now for the hard part."

Evan dialed the number very carefully. "Hello?"

Evan fixed his eyes on the horizon and sat up a little straighter. "Mom, it's me. Sue Ann and I are in love, and we're going to get married."

Another parental pause.

"Evan, if you marry that young woman, you'll have no home to come back to."

"I'm sorry, Mom. I love her, and she loves me." The phone line went dead, and Evan and I turned our pleading eyes toward my aunt.

"Pul-lease," we both begged in unison.

My aunt threw up her hands and laughed. "Who am I to stop young love? I'll go call the minister."

❧❧❧

"I'm not pregnant."

"Oh." Evan's face looked both relieved and scared. It meant we had married prematurely. If we had only waited two more weeks, we could have avoided the whole thing, but the doctor seemed so certain. "I guess that means we can save a bit more from my paycheck when I join the Navy."

"Yeah, I guess so." I brightened at the next thought. "And I can keep working at my job!" I worked at a local hangout joint as a waitress, and I adored my job because all my friends came to see me. It proved to be the perfect environment for an extrovert like me to be employed.

My husband smiled at my happiness. "That's right, honey. Don't worry, the family will come in time." Only a few months later, that came true.

Soon after, Evan was stationed in San Diego, and I made the lonely trek out to join him. Feeling nauseous with morning sickness and extra hormones, I arrived at the little apartment where Evan and I were to live only to discover that Evan was confined to the base, and I would spend the first months completely by myself.

The apartment, located in the city just a few miles off base, bordered on the ghetto. Unsure of my surroundings and the new life I carried, I was fit to be tied. To make matters worse, there was a discrepancy with Evan's paycheck, and I had zero access to money. With no food in the house, I didn't know what to do other than walk the 52 blocks to the Red Cross for help.

Reaching my limit, I finally got word to Evan that I couldn't bear living in San Diego, and I wanted to go home. He arranged for a flight back to our hometown, and I boarded the plane without a dime. I had to borrow one from the soldier who sat next to me in order to call my parents when we landed. The phone rang and rang before I realized they weren't home. Desperate, I called Evan's mother. Despite her threats to disown Evan when he married me, she came and picked me up and took me out to eat.

"I'm pregnant, Mrs. Roberts," I finally revealed over a hearty dinner at a diner.

Her eyes squinted tightly together for a moment, as if to shield herself from the reality of my statement. "I see. Well, I suppose we'll have to do all the right things, then."

That was the extent of our conversation, although the tension between us lightened, and she seemed to warm up to me a little more. She dropped me at my parents' home, and after digging around for the spare key in the flower pot and letting myself inside, I fell across my bed. How could I have ended up like this? An unwanted marriage to a man I never saw, an unbearable living situation and now a child for whom I was not prepared? I cried myself into a deep sleep.

I awoke to light flutters in my stomach. "What's this?" I said aloud and grasped my belly with both hands. The flutters grew all the more intense, and I realized their significance. "My baby!" I sat up in utter delight. "It's moving!"

Tears rolled down my cheeks, but these were tears of joy. The sorrow and uncertainty melted away, unveiling a love for this mysterious being I had never felt before. I arose from the bed and made my way into the kitchen, twirling around and singing, "I am going to love you forever. Forever and always my baby you'll be!" My parents often told me I couldn't carry a tune in a bucket, but I didn't care.

When my parents arrived home later, they found me in high spirits. After hearing about my nightmarish experience in San Diego, we all agreed I should move back home until Evan returned in a few months. Then we could get an apartment close by and settle down.

꩜꩜꩜

"One, two, three, push! You're doing great, Sue Ann! A few more pushes, and that baby is going to help me win that bet." Dr. Casey flashed me a grin.

I tried to smile, but all I could manage was a grunt as I mustered up enough strength for another push. Dr. Casey was right. A few more pushes and DeeDee entered the world. At 6 pounds, 14 ounces, she was every bit the perfection I imagined her to be. I couldn't take my eyes off of her. Days went by with us just staring at each other — completely enraptured — and laughing and playing.

Since Evan was away, my dad often swung by to check in on his girls, as he would say. "The dishes are stacked in the sink, and it looks like she hasn't tidied the house in years," my dad grinned as he reported my state to my mother. "But nothing else matters to her except playing with that baby." My mom would sigh at the thought of such a disheveled living environment and make a mental note to come and help me on the weekends.

But DeeDee and I didn't need any help. Together, we formed a perfect and whole universe. DeeDee never crawled. At 8 months, she walked and began to speak. When Evan finally returned home on leave, he was flabbergasted. At 9 months, this was the first time he had laid eyes on her.

"Oh, Sue Ann, she's beautiful."

I beamed with maternal pride. "She's perfection," I agreed.

We watched her for a few moments before the conversation turned to other things.

"They're shipping me out to San Diego again." His eyes looked at me pleadingly. "If I find you a nicer home, will you come?"

"Of course." My voice faltered, but only for a moment. "I'm your wife, Evan. We're in this together."

It was Evan's turn to beam as he pulled me into a stifling embrace.

༂ఄ༂ఄ༂ఄ

Evan did indeed find us a nicer home outside San Diego in a place called Chula Vista. We settled in a duplex in a non-military community with a pool. Then Evan was sent off, and I found myself on my own again. DeeDee and I made friends easily, and our next-door neighbors turned out to be avid partiers. I had been exposed to drugs and alcohol before, but not at this level. And I didn't know how to stop drinking once I started. In fact, every time I did drink, I became ill. But I thought that was normal, that everyone became falling-down drunk when he or she drank. With Evan traveling, drinking made it easier for me to socialize. And my drinking habit stuck even when he did return.

"You shouldn't drink that much," he would say mildly and then drop the subject before it evolved into an argument.

Though everything seemed picture-perfect on the exterior, Evan's and my marriage deteriorated. Raised in a conservative home, Evan showed very little affection for me outside of the bedroom. Bent on establishing himself and saving money, it was difficult to draw him out and have a little fun. My mother once sent him money to take me to a nice restaurant, and Evan instead drove me to a nearby KFC and put the rest of the money in his pocket. Perhaps my drinking was the only outlet for exuberance I could find.

The marriage lasted five years. In 1970, I went in for surgery for a cyst on my tailbone. Evan was not scheduled to come home at that time, and I wrote him a letter to prepare him before he returned to be with me.

"When you come, please don't think things are the same between us, because they're not," I had included in the closing lines. After he read the letter, the Navy let him out early, and he was able to come home.

Two days after the surgery, I filed for divorce. Evan's father's attorney served him the papers. I told no one, especially my parents, because I knew they didn't believe in divorce. It seems silly now, but I thought I could keep it a secret for a while. Evan, however, thought differently. He immediately informed my parents, perhaps in a last-ditch effort to salvage the marriage. The attempt failed, and we finalized the divorce in 1971. I received custody of DeeDee. Evan married Natalie a few days later and filed for full custody.

෨෨෨෨

"Honey, the phone's for you. It sounds like Evan," my dad called. I emerged from the pile of laundry I was cleaning and picked up the phone.

"Hello?"

"Sue Ann, it's Evan."

"Hi, Evan," I said politely.

"Sue Ann, we just got custody of DeeDee. We'll be over shortly to pick her up."

The words hit me like dead weight. "Over my dead body!" I slammed the phone down and ran to fetch my suitcase.

My father gave me a funny look. "What's happening, Sue Ann?"

I didn't slow down to explain. "It's Evan and Natalie. They've gotten custody of DeeDee, and they're coming over in a few minutes to get her."

My father turned pale. He picked up the phone and dialed my brother. "Richard, I need you over here right now," he barked.

My mother looked as though she might faint when she heard the news, but she straightened up and dug through her purse to retrieve $50 and a gas credit card. She pressed them into my hand without a word, before running off to collect more clothes for my suitcase. It felt like an eternity, but the car was packed in a matter of minutes after hanging up with Evan. My brother arrived to escort me out of town — just to be sure no one was following me.

I drove until I reached La Grande, Oregon, about 300 miles east of Dallas. I found an apartment and a job at Vip's Lounge as a bartender. During the interview, I informed my boss that I was on the run. He looked at me a good minute before replying, "No problem. We're all on the run from something."

It took Evan six months and $6,000 to find me. Finally, they subpoenaed my mother's phone records and discovered a string of collect calls from La Grande. Hot on the trail, they continued their investigation until they found out where I worked. Then it was merely a game of cat and mouse. I left DeeDee with the babysitter, and as my new boyfriend and I drove home, the police pulled in behind us. Two officers exited the vehicle and approached me. "Are you Sue Ann Roberts?"

My boyfriend immediately moved around to my side of the vehicle and put his arm around me. "Yes," I replied as calmly as possible.

"We have to arrest you."

I silently offered up my wrists, they cuffed me and then drove me down to the police station. When we arrived, the detective gave me a long, hard look. "Ma'am, you've got to 'fess up as to the whereabouts of your daughter. You're facing some pretty hard charges, and they will only get worse if you refuse to cooperate."

I sat there for a long time and contemplated my options. I knew I couldn't run anymore, and I knew that Evan, powered by Natalie's spitefulness, would not be forgiving. My lips quivered, but my voice remained calm as I responded. "She's at the babysitter's house."

"Why don't you take us there?" the officer suggested in a gentler voice. We got in the car, and I gave them the directions. When we arrived, the babysitter placed DeeDee in my arms and embraced the two of us together. "We're pulling for you," she whispered. "Lord knows, this little girl needs her mother." Then we drove back to the station. DeeDee and I remained upstairs until word came that Evan and Natalie had arrived; then the two police officers escorted us down to a room where the exchange would take place. DeeDee remained calm until that point, and then she began to scream, "Mommy, I want to stay here with you. Please don't make me go!"

"Oh, sweetie, I would never make you leave me. I love you so very, very much. But the court has decided that you should live with Daddy and Natalie for a little while."

DeeDee buried her head in my skirt and cried. "No, Mama, that isn't right. I need to live with you. You're my mommy."

I lifted up her precious face so that our eyes met and said, "I am going to do everything in my power to have you here with me."

          ≈≈≈

Natalie and Evan eventually arrived, and the exchange took place. After traveling to Dallas to face my court charges, I returned to La Grande, my job at Vip's and my boyfriend. Every other week, I took a bus to Dallas, my father picked me up and we drove to Evan and Natalie's home to pick up DeeDee. We did this for a year, until 1974 when I moved to Eugene, Oregon, in order to be closer to DeeDee. I found another job bartending and partied like a rock star. I used to frequent other bars so that my customers would not see me inebriated.

During all of this, Evan and I were in and out of court in a battle just to keep my visitation rights for our daughter. I don't know how many lawyers I didn't pay in those seven years.

I had very little income as a waitress and bartender, but I couldn't sit back and allow my child to be raised by another woman, especially one with as much hatefulness and spite as Natalie.

After several years of court battles, one lawyer finally called my husband to the stand for questioning. Since Evan was home very little during the visitations because of his work, he glanced repeatedly at Natalie, who was in the audience, for answers. The judge caught on quickly. "Mr. Roberts, he's asking you that question, not the lady in the audience."

Evan lowered his eyes. "I'm sorry, Your Honor."

"Now answer the question."

"I don't know, Your Honor."

"You don't know," the judge repeated and paused for a moment. "It seems to me, Mr. Roberts, that you know very little about what transpires during these visitations. Though I can't fault you for having to work, I can change the structure of the visitations to better accommodate your ex-wife, who seems to be suffering terribly at the hands of the lady in the audience. Therefore, I rule that there is to be no more communication between the ex-Mrs. Roberts and the present Mrs. Roberts. All communication should flow between the ex-Mrs. Roberts and Mr. Roberts only. Failure to do so will result in contempt of court. Furthermore, all future visitations will occur at the home of the ex-Mrs. Roberts' parents. This court is adjourned."

సొసొసొ

"Have you looked in the newspaper?" my father asked me one night over dinner at the Elks Lodge. My hours had dwindled to almost nothing at the restaurant where I worked, and I needed to find more quickly.

"Yes, but it's the same old, same old. No new opportunities ever present themselves."

I sighed dramatically before continuing. "I don't know, Dad. I'm 29. I guess I'm looking for one last adventure before I turn 30 and get old." My dad laughed.

"You are definitely getting up there," he kidded.

A man, sitting nearby, turned to me. "Well, I own a fishing lodge. Would that suit you?"

My eyes widened in delight at a new adventure. "Really, Mister?"

"Call me Bob," the man replied warmly. "And, yes, I own a fishing lodge in Alaska, and I need a few more hospitality workers. You know, making up the rooms, setting the tables for meals, packing lunches for excursions … it's only for the summer now, but it may get you over that hump."

"Oh, Bob, that would be wonderful!" I was ecstatic. I looked at my dad, but I knew he'd go for it.

"Why don't you give your mom a call and ask her?"

"Darn it," I said. "I know exactly what she'll have to say about it."

"Go on, honey. Here, take this dime, and see what she says."

Reluctantly, I dialed her number. "Hello?"

I rallied myself and dove into my spiel. "Mom, guess what? I've found a job at a fishing lodge in Alaska!"

"Sue Ann, I think that is just horrible. That is ridiculous for a young woman to do. What on earth are you going to be doing?"

"Hospitality, Mom." I emphasized the word to give it more weight. "Besides it's just for the summer."

My mother sighed when she realized I had made up my mind. "You're going to need some help getting up there. Besides that you're getting sickly looking. Your father and I want you to come back home for a while, anyway. So if you come and stay with us for this next month, we'll help you in the way of clothes. Alaskan weather is different from Oregon's."

I nearly did a cartwheel. "Oh, thank you, Mom!" I hung up and bounded back to my father and Bob.

"She said, 'If you think you have to,'" I told them sarcastically. I bear hugged my father and shook Bob's hand.

"Here's my card. Call me, and we'll set up a flight for you and get your information."

"Thank you so much!"

"Here's to your adventure."

A VERITABLE JOY

ৡৡৡ

I followed my mother's instructions to a T, gave up my apartment and moved back in with them. I even put my partying on hold so that I wouldn't look so sickly. My parents took me shopping for clothes, and within two weeks, I boarded a plane to Alaska. It was a glorious summer. The lodge sat in a valley surrounded by majestic mountains that overlooked the lake. People from all over the world traveled to catch a glimpse of the great salmon, the Kodiak bears and the lush, breathtaking topography. The constant ebb and flow of travelers, the international flair of the lodge and the beauty of the surroundings appealed to all of my senses. I felt fiercely independent for the first time in my life.

As the summer ended, and signs of autumn began to manifest in the trees and temperature, the idea of returning to my dull life in Dallas, Oregon, held little, if any, appeal.

As I was tidying up the kitchen one day, Bob found me. "Well, young lady, how did you like your stay here?"

"Oh, Bob, you know I loved every minute of it. I don't know how I can go back to Dallas after meeting so many wonderful people and living in such a beautiful place. You and the rest of the staff have become like family to me."

Bob patted my hand reassuringly. "I thought you might have gone and fallen in love with this place. You've been a wonderful part of our team here, and I am sorry I can't offer you a more permanent job, but I know you have commitments back in Dallas that need attending. Still, there are a few more weeks of warm weather. I'll tell you what: If you can beat me 2:3 at cribbage, I'll give you two weeks at my condo in Hawaii. That should help get Alaska out of your blood."

Once again, my eyes widened at the prospect of another exotic place. "You have yourself a deal!"

Bob must have let me win because I hadn't the faintest idea how to play cribbage, and word around the lodge was that he played a tough game. The next week I bid a tearful adieu to Alaska and flew to Hawaii. Bob was right: The change of scenery helped assuage the pain of leaving the lodge. Besides, I secretly made a pact with myself that I would one day return.

๛๛๛

When I arrived home, I found another apartment and a job bartending at the Ponderosa Lounge. Visitations with my daughter resumed, as did my extensive drinking and partying.

One night, as I worked in the lounge, a man came into the bar who took my breath away. As a teen, I used to dream about a tall man with dark hair and blue eyes leaning in for a kiss, and here he was — 15 years later and looking every bit as fine as I had imagined.

"Hi." He flashed me an absolutely gorgeous smile and sat down directly in front of me. "I'll have a highball with Parker's Heritage, please."

I nodded and began to prepare the drink. I almost forgot how to make it, I was so busy staring at him. He seemed interested in me as well.

"So …" he finally said, and we exchanged a few coy sentences. "How would you feel if I took you out for dinner?"

"I don't date my customers. Besides, I don't even know your name."

"It's Pierce."

"Nice to meet you. I'm Sue Ann."

"Well, Sue Ann, what do I have to do to convince you to go out with me? Take my business elsewhere? Change bars? Go across the street, call you up and ask you out?"

I laughed. "Okay, enough with the questions. I'll go out with you!"

We spent the rest of the night deep in conversation. In fact, he closed the bar with me. After everything I went through with Evan, I never would have dreamt it possible, but I fell head over heels in love with him. Love at first sight — it was the real deal. And he felt the same about me.

Four weeks later, in the fall of 1976, Pierce and I flew to Reno and married. I carried him over the threshold. We moved to Central Point, Oregon, into a little apartment with a corral in the back. Pierce was a cowboy and kept two horses, Shadow and Charlie.

Pierce and I reveled in our newfound love. He taught me to ride horses and spent many evenings dreaming with me about buying a ranch and growing old together. We also did our share of partying. Pierce liked his whiskey, and between the two of us, our collection of empty liquor bottles multiplied like rabbits. I also learned that Pierce didn't like to hear about my past. He became very jealous and very vocal quickly, especially when he was drinking.

Slowly our marriage devolved from one based on passion and affection, to one that centered on alcohol and partying.

Even though I drank a lot whenever we partied, I did not need to drink every day. I simply didn't know how to quit completely. Pierce, however, liked his whiskey every day.

కకకక

"I got the job," Pierce announced over dinner one night.

"Really, so we're moving to Alaska?" I couldn't believe it — my return to Alaska was finally imminent.

"Yes, my dear, to a logging camp called Thorne Bay on Prince of Wales Island." Pierce reached for my hand. "And it's a dry camp."

"Really?"

"This might be a good time for us — me, at least — to quit drinking. What do you think?"

I nodded solemnly, and my heart gave a leap in the hope that sobriety could be a reality. "When do we leave?"

"The job starts at summer's end. That gives us a few months to pack up the house and —"

"Find a solution for DeeDee. Rumor has it that Evan and Natalie aren't getting along. If Evan divorces her ..." I couldn't finish the sentence without a catch in my throat.

"We're going to give her the best life imaginable. Especially after all she's been through."

᚛᚛᚛

Evan did indeed file for divorce a few weeks later. With Natalie finally out of the picture, I had a long conversation with Evan.

In full agreement that DeeDee should make her own decision, I invited DeeDee to come and live with Pierce and me for the summer. It was the most joyful reunion I had ever experienced.

At the end of the summer, I sat with DeeDee in the kitchen. "DeeDee, Natalie is gone and no longer has a say regarding where you live or with whom. Your father and I have spoken, and we realize that, at 12 years old, you are perfectly capable of deciding where you'd like to live. You know Pierce and I are moving to Alaska in a few weeks, so there would be a lot of changes for you — a new family, a new place, a new school. But I know you will do wonderfully, if that's where you choose to be."

DeeDee sat in silence for a long time. "I want to live with you, Mom."

I stifled a sigh of relief, mingled with intense thankfulness. "Well, you have to tell your dad that."

"I'm afraid to — I don't want to hurt his feelings."

"Oh, honey, it'll be really easy. Your dad wants you to make that decision."

"Okay, but can you help me?"

"Of course, babycakes." Each of us picked up a receiver, and I dialed Evan's number.

"Evan? Hi, this is Sue Ann and DeeDee. We've been talking, and DeeDee has some news she wants to share with you."

"Hi, DeeDee."

"Hi, Dad. It's just that …" DeeDee's voice trailed off as she struggled to find the least offensive words.

"It's okay, honey," Evan said softly. "I support whatever you decide, and you know I will always love you. Your mom and I want the very best for you."

DeeDee's eyes glistened with tears. "I love you, Dad, so much, but I think I want to live with Mom right now."

"Sweetie, that is perfectly fine! Your mom and you have been apart for so long, and I think you need a little time together."

"Really, Dad? You're not upset?"

"Not in the least, honey."

DeeDee smiled through her tears. "Thanks, Dad. I love you."

"Love you, too."

DeeDee hung up the phone, and she and I fell into an embrace laughing and crying. Mother and daughter could finally be together.

శ్రీశ్రీశ్రీ

A VERITABLE JOY

At the end of August, DeeDee, Pierce and I moved to Thorne Bay. Arriving by float plane, with our belongings stowed away in a ferry, we were assigned a home that overlooked the bay. I enrolled DeeDee in school, and Pierce got to work. I kept house and threw myself into being a mother.

Unfortunately, the logging camp was not the dry place we were led to believe it was. In fact, there was more carousing on the island than I had seen in a long time. Instead of sobering up and assuming more responsibility now that we had DeeDee, Pierce and I continued to party, and verbal and physical abuse began to trickle into our relationship. Pierce was unfaithful, and our marriage went into rapid decline.

కాకాకా

"What can I do for you today?" I asked, forcing a smile and trying to avoid blindness from the sunlight pouring in through my door. It had been a long previous night, and I hadn't anticipated any visitors before noon.

"Hi, Sue Ann. I don't think we've formally met, but my name is Rob, and I'm the pastor at the little church here at the camp."

"Oh, hello. Won't you come in?"

"Thank you, I'd like that."

I made two mugs of coffee, and we sat in the living room. "Do you know about Jesus?" He asked the question suddenly, without any preface, and it caught me off guard.

"Yes, yes, of course. I prayed to Jesus once at a Mennonite Baptist church."

"Did you invite him to be a part of your life?"

"I did, but it hasn't seemed to take very well. There are things about my life I'd like to change."

"Like what?" The pastor seemed more caring than nosy, and I found myself disclosing past hurts, my struggle with alcohol and my wounded marriage.

"You know, if you ask Jesus to come and help you with those things, he will be faithful to put you into situations that will bring healing."

"Really?" I said with just a hint of sarcasm. "Because I could really use some healing now."

"Why don't we pray?"

I thought for a moment. My marriage was crumbling in pieces around me, I had no idea how to drink without becoming completely intoxicated and DeeDee was in the throes of adolescence. What did I have to lose? With a nod of my head, I folded my hands and closed my eyes like I remembered seeing in old movies.

"You can repeat after me, if you'd like."

"Jesus, I'm sorry for the wrong I've done in my life."

"Jesus, I'm sorry for the wrong I've done in my life."

"And I invite you to be a part of my life and live in my heart."

"And I invite you to be a part of my life and live in my heart."

"Amen."

"Amen? That's it?"

"That's it!"

Pastor Rob rose to leave. "You are welcome any time at our church, Sue Ann, and I will be praying for you as you learn to trust God to lead you."

"Thank you, Rob."

৯৯৯

I never attended Rob's church, but soon after, I did meet Joanie. She was 29 years old and already had more than a decade of sobriety. There was an AA chapter that met in the camp, and knowing that I needed help, I started going when Joanie invited me. The group felt very accepting and comfortable to me, despite the fact that I clearly communicated I wasn't ready to stop drinking.

I still needed an outlet to deal with the infidelity and abuse in my marriage. Pierce physically assaulted me when I threatened to leave, and I came to the realization that leaving was no longer an option. I began taking the occasional babysitting job so that I could save up some get-away cash. During one of my jobs, I ran into a Forest Service Ranger, and he and I struck up a conversation. Getting the drift that I was in a bad spot with my marriage, he said, "You know, I could get you off the island. I am going on a two-week sheep hunting trip in Northern British Columbia. You could go along as my guest, if you like."

Two weeks would be exactly what I needed to escape Pierce's wrath. By the time I came back, he would be calm enough to reason with. DeeDee was away at a fine arts camp and would be home in a few days, but I could fly her out to see her grandparents. "Alright, I'll go."

I returned home and planned my escape. I called my parents and then DeeDee to tell her she could go straight to Grandma's instead of coming home. The hardest part I saved for last.

"Joanie, hi. This is Sue Ann."

"Hi, Sue Ann! Are you coming over tonight? I'll cook!"

"That sounds wonderful, but actually ..." I swallowed hard. "Joanie, I am leaving Pierce."

"What —"

"I met a guy who's going to get me off the island for the next two weeks. That should give Pierce enough time to calm down. I need you to take care of him, Joanie. He's not going to take this well."

Joanie let out a low whistle. "You're right. I will make sure he's okay. And Sue Ann? Be safe."

"Thanks! I'll miss you all. See you soon."

The next day while Pierce was at work, the Forest Service Ranger stopped by, and I threw a few suitcases in the back of his truck. He left, and I waited until the following day to take the ferry off the island. He met me at the dock, and we spent the next two weeks riding horseback through the Rocky Mountains. I made great friends with the cook, and we invented delicious recipes while the fellows were off hunting. The day before I left, I called Joanie.

"How's Pierce?"

"Pierce decided to go through treatment. He's in Idaho."

Floored but thankful, I hung up.

The next day, we headed home. Just as we drove up to the dock, a float plane landed, and Pierce got out. When he saw me with another man, all hell broke loose. The Forest Service Ranger handed me his gun and went out to meet Pierce. A ring of onlookers quickly formed, and when I realized that only I could stop the fight, I raised the gun in the air and fired.

"Alright, you two. Either you stop the fight, or I stop the fight!"

Both men stood at attention. "You're coming home with me right now," growled Pierce.

"No, I am not." I stood my ground. "I will come up there. But I am going to make sure he's alright. You're misunderstanding this whole thing."

Pierce turned away and stomped up to the house. When I joined him, he said, "I want to make a go of it."

I shook my head. "Pierce, my gut says no. You go through treatment, and I'll go to Juneau. We don't have to lose contact. If things go well, maybe we can talk about getting back together."

❧❧❧

Pierce returned to Idaho for treatment, and I flew to Juneau with nothing but $600 to my name. I got a hotel for a few days. Walking around with no permanent residence and no job, I decided to find an AA meeting. After the meeting concluded, a barber approached me. "You know, I have a friend who has a room in a mobile home for rent for $150 per week. Why don't you borrow my car and go take a look at it?"

"Are you sure? You don't even know me, and you'll let me borrow your car? Is this place even close to town?"

The man laughed. "Honey, there are only 45 miles of road in Juneau. Where you going to go?"

A few days later, I was all moved in. The Latch String Dining Room and Lounge at the Baranof Hotel hired me as a server. Grateful for the offer, but knowing that DeeDee would be arriving in a few weeks for school, I told them I would have to continue looking for a day job. There was no way I was going to be able to work nights while raising a teenager. The manager looked at me and smiled. "You're a fantastic server, Sue Ann, and I wish we could keep you. But maybe you should talk to Barbara in the office. I think she's looking for an assistant."

Barbara hired me for one of my first 9-to-5 jobs ever. I was thrilled and drank to my heart's content. In fact, I spent the weekend drinking — so much, that I was late for work on Monday. Barbara didn't appear to mind, though. She drank as well and understood the difficulty with early hours. Being late on Monday became one of my favorite habits, so much so, that when I finally managed to get myself in on time, Barbara sent me a dozen red roses with "Congratulations!" scrawled across the card.

I found an apartment just before DeeDee arrived, and

we began our new life. Everything was going along fine until October.

"Hello?"

"Hi."

"Pierce, how are things? How's treatment?"

"Really good, really good … except I miss you. I'm ready to give it another try again, only this time, I'll be sober."

My stomach sank. "I don't know, Pierce. It's only been a few months. Don't you want to wait a little longer?"

"I can't, baby. We need to be together. Please?"

"Fine," I relented. "But when you come, you come as my roommate, not as my husband."

"Okay."

We lasted nine months before Pierce picked me up and threw me into a chair in an argument. It was too hard with him sober and me still drinking. I took out a restraining order on him for a week and then drove him to the airport. He had received a grant to attend school for social work in Utah. I filed for a 30-day $50 divorce in the summer of 1982.

꙳꙳꙳

"Mom! Mom, wake up!" My daughter shook me vigorously until I grunted, indicating that I was indeed alive. I opened my eyes and looked up at the ceiling that bridged the bathroom and living area. Then my eyes fell on my daughter.

The anger and concern were apparent on her face. "I thought you were dead! What did you do last night?"

I sat up and thought very hard for a moment. "Well, the last thing I remember was pouring some Grand Marnier into a soda can and heading out to take the bus from Juneau to Auke Bay to hang out with Agnes."

"Really? In a soda can? That is so high school, Mom." We didn't speak much the rest of the afternoon, but I knew DeeDee could tell I had a problem. That bothered me. I didn't like DeeDee knowing that her mother was a drunk. Still, I couldn't let go. I even took on a weekend job tending a bar in Auke Bay, just so I could drink for free.

〨〨〨〨

"May I see your license, please, ma'am?" After digging around in my purse for what seemed like an eternity, I cracked my window four inches and slid the document through. I kept my face down and my mouth shut.

Boy, you're in trouble now, I said to myself. The guy in the passenger seat was not at all quiet. Bubbling over with inebriation, he talked non-stop.

"Oh, my gosh, I am so drunk! Thank God she's driving me home. I couldn't walk a straight line even if it meant my li —"

"Okay, you're good to go," the officer interrupted him and passed me back my license.

I clutched it gratefully in my hand and put it carefully in my purse. My friend and I had been drinking straight shots of tequila since 3 in the afternoon. Now, well after 2 a.m., we were headed to his house to drop a few lines of coke. We had both been so drunk, we had to lean on each other to keep from falling down as we exited the bar. Somehow, he convinced me to drive. I don't really remember that part or the 13-mile drive into Juneau, but I do recall the red lights pulling up behind us as soon as we turned onto the main road.

The next morning, I called a friend from AA to come and pick me up. She asked me for directions, and I couldn't tell her to save my life. I had to put the guy I had been drinking with on the phone, and he told her the way there. She drove me back to her house, where I showered and then slept the rest of the day. I awoke in the late afternoon to the sounds of laughter and conversation.

"Hello?" I called out from the bedroom nice and loudly so she would know I was up.

"Hey!" she said, peeking around the door.

"Who's out there?" I wanted to use the bathroom, which required a walk through the living area, and I didn't want anyone to see me like this. My permed hair lay against my head and came up to a point like a teepee. My face was un-made-up, and my eyes were red from too much alcohol. I was definitely not ready for my close-up.

"Oh, just our friends from AA. You can come on out — you know we all love you."

After an unsuccessful attempt to smooth down my hair, I followed her into the great room.

"Hey, Sue Ann, how's it going?" They all seemed so

cheerful and happy. And they were genuinely glad to see me, in spite of my condition.

"Hey!" I gave a wave. "I'll be right out." I walked to the bathroom and fixed myself up a bit and then joined the rest of the group. We talked for several hours before heading to our homes. As we got ready to leave, one of the guys came up to me and placed his hand on my shoulder.

"Sue Ann," he said gently. "When you first came to AA, I thought, 'There is no way she is an alcoholic. She's too well put together.' But today, I have to tell you, you look like s***. Today you fit the bill of a drunk."

"I know," I replied, "but today I don't want to hear it because I'm not ready to come back to AA." However, I did hear him loud and clear. As I walked out the door, a plan formulated in my mind: Go sober on New Year's.

❧❧❧

New Year's Eve rolled around quickly. I got off work and ordered two peppermint schnapps, just so I could say I had a drink. Then I drove home and prepared myself to celebrate the New Year at the Alano Club with my AA friends. On New Year's Day, I absentmindedly smoked a joint with one of my friends, but I've been clean of alcohol and drugs since then. I also committed myself to my AA group. I referred to myself as their puppet because I did whatever they suggested and accepted their discipline. I trusted them and felt at home with them because they did not judge me. I attended 400 AA meetings in 1983 alone.

My friends call me a high-bottom drunk because I didn't suffer many physical withdrawal symptoms — I guess because I didn't drink every day. However, I definitely suffered emotional withdrawal. A funny thing happened, though. When I stopped drinking, my emotions began to pour out of me. All the feelings I had bottled up from when I was a little girl, to my first marriage, to Natalie came tumbling out.

As I purged emotionally, I came to the realization that I needed to forgive Natalie. All these years, I deemed her the driving force behind DeeDee's and my separation and, ultimately, my drinking. When they took DeeDee away, I felt robbed of the right of my motherhood and thus an integral element of my identity. Only drinking diluted the hatred I felt toward her, until Jesus began to permeate my life through the love and compassion of others. His love for me displaced the need for alcohol and, with it, the negative emotions I harbored. I started to ask Jesus for the strength to forgive her, but the words refused to come. So I called a friend from AA.

"I've got to forgive Natalie, but I can't. Can you help me?"

"Sure! Why don't I start us out, and you can take over when you feel ready?"

"That would be great."

"Lord, we come to you today because we know your desire is for us to live a life free of hatred and unforgiveness. We know Sue Ann wants to honor you, and we ask you to send your Holy Spirit to help her unlock and release the feelings she has in her heart toward Natalie. So today, we ask you to help Sue Ann forgive Natalie. She chooses to let go of the pain and suffering that Natalie caused in her life. She releases Natalie and will not exact retribution, but will bless Natalie. We declare Sue Ann free from the need to get revenge and free to live out her life according to your plan, God. In Jesus' name, Amen."

I tilted my head back and opened my arms. It felt as though God had removed a great weight from my shoulders. I felt invigorated and joyful.

❧ ❧ ❧

"DeeDee, Grandpa is sick, and I need to go be with him. I've arranged for you to stay at your friend's house, and I'll be back in a few days."

"What happened, Mom?" My daughter's voice filled with concern. How she loved her Grandpa. He had been a fun and loving constant in her life for so many years.

"He had another heart attack. They said it was a miracle he lived through the first one, but I'm not sure about this one …" My voice trailed off, and I put my head in my hands.

"Is he going to make it? Can I come with you? Please, I need to see him."

I shrugged. "Sweetie, I had to borrow money for my ticket, and even though I want to, I can't afford two tickets. And I need to be there to help Grandma."

"But, Mom, what if he — what if he — doesn't make it?"

"DeeDee, we're going to believe that he'll be okay and that you'll see him again." I hugged her close. "Now I need you to pack a suitcase for your friend's house. I'm taking the red-eye out tonight."

I barely arrived in time. My father passed hours later. We cremated his body and, according to his wishes, snuck over to the Elks Lodge and spread his ashes behind the building. "So I can be with my buddies," he had said when we questioned his reasoning.

I knew DeeDee would be heartbroken that she never saw him. In retrospect, my problems with DeeDee began after my father passed. Out of anger that her request to see her grandfather was denied, she began to rebel.

తతతత

The year passed quickly. That summer, I lost my job because of a back injury that put me in bed for two weeks. My boss, Barbara, and I cried at the thought of parting ways, but I felt at peace about it because I could draw unemployment and work more diligently on my recovery.

In August, I received a call in the middle of the night that DeeDee had been admitted to the ER for some sort of drug overdose. I rushed over to the hospital. "What happened?"

The doctor looked tired and perplexed. "We know she overdosed, but we can't seem to identify the drug. We really need to know what she took in order to detox her properly."

"Where did you find her?"

"She was out with a couple of friends at the skating rink."

"Give me about 15 minutes, and I'll have your answer." I made a beeline for the parking lot and practically sped toward the skating rink on two tires. I jumped out of the car and ran inside. After a quick glance around the building, I located one of DeeDee's friends in the bathroom.

"Oh, hi, Mrs. —"

"Listen, you little punk," I interrupted her and lowered my face very close to hers as I backed her up against the wall. "I'm not here to bring you in. In fact, I don't care what you've been up to, but I sure as h*** care what my daughter puts in her body. Now, either you tell me, or I call your mom and dad."

The girl was so afraid, she whispered the name of the drug in my ear. "Thank you," I said curtly and ran back to my car.

DeeDee was just beginning to come off of the drug when I returned to the hospital. The nurse recognized the drug right away and began preparing the detox. I borrowed her phone and put in a call to my friend who ran the treatment center directly behind the hospital.

"I'm calling in a favor, George. DeeDee has taken some sort of hallucinogen, and I need to be certain this is the last time she even thinks about touching drugs."

"Well, the treatment center is not really for teens, and the patient has to voluntarily commit herself. However, DeeDee doesn't have to know that. And I could have the drunk wagon pick her up. That would really seal the deal."

I stifled a giggle. "You mean the one they use to collect all the drunk people from off the streets?"

"The very one."

"I love it! Let's do it."

When DeeDee awoke, I asked her if she knew her location and why she was there. When I heard that she did, I told her I would see her in three days and left. DeeDee never touched another drug again.

જ્જ્જ

In November, DeeDee attempted to move out on her own with a bunch of friends, but they kicked her out just in time for Christmas.

My mother visited us that year, and we had a lovely holiday, just the three of us. As my mom's visit neared its end, we decided to go shopping. As we passed a couple on the street, they waved.

"Hi, Sue Ann! It's great to see you."

"Thanks," I said, feeling a little bewildered. I didn't really know them all that well. He was a fairly infamous drug dealer, and I recognized his wife from AA meetings.

"We're so looking forward to having DeeDee come live with us for a while."

"Excuse me?"

"Yeah, she didn't tell you? She came to us and asked if we had a spare room."

"Wow. Okay, I really appreciate you telling me. You guys take care now."

"Bye." They waved and continued on their way.

I stopped dead in my tracks. "Did you hear that, Mom?"

"Unbelievable. And you really had no idea?"

"None, but now that I do, I think I need to have a conversation with Evan."

"Good idea."

That evening, Evan and I talked for a long while about how to best help our daughter. Evan had since married a wonderful woman named Linda. Though I hated to let her go, I knew they could provide her with the stability she needed to live a healthy and happy life. We made arrangements. I took the $1,000 I had won at a BINGO night and bought a ticket on the same return flight as my mother's. I even booked them next to each other. When DeeDee came in the house, I asked her to go for a ride with me. I pulled into the driveway of the couple where she was to move. "Do you want me to get your stuff or do you want to? You're going home to your dad's."

A brief argument ensued, which I won, and then together we went in and collected her things. Then I brought her home and made sure she stayed there until I could put her on the plane. DeeDee refused to speak to me, and she didn't hug me goodbye, but I knew I was doing the right thing.

A VERITABLE JOY

༚༚༚

New Year's passed quietly and a little lonely without my family around me. I celebrated my one year of sobriety with my AA friends. In February, the boiler went out in my apartment, and the landlord put us up in a hotel. One evening, as I lay across the bed, an uncertainty about the future crept into my mind. I turned off the TV and tried to focus on what my next step should be. As I lay there, I heard a voice say, "You need to move."

"What?" I sat up and looked around for the speaker.

"You need to move."

"Okay, God, I think that's you, and I am going to listen."

I called my mother and asked her if she wanted a roommate. Then I packed my belongings and booked a flight to Dallas.

༚༚༚

It took DeeDee two or three months to come around, but her rebellious side softened with the love and support of her dad, Linda, her grandmother and me. She dropped out of school, but Linda, who had never finished high school, encouraged DeeDee to go back to school with her and get her GED. Both of them graduated in the summer of 1984. Evan, Linda, Pierce, Evan's parents, my mother and I were all in attendance to celebrate DeeDee's and Linda's accomplishments.

પ્રઙ્ફ

Life settled down some after that summer. A bar hired me to bartend. The other bartender, Teresa, and I became fast friends, along with the music manager.

"I notice you like to sing along with the band while you work," he said to me one evening as we closed down the bar.

"Yeah, I love to sing. It's a shame I like to do something I'm so bad at — people always told me I couldn't carry a tune in a bucket."

"Hmm. That's not the way I hear it. The truth is, you're pretty good. I was wondering if one of these days, like maybe tomorrow evening, you'd come up and sing with the band?"

I stopped wiping down the bar and stared at him. "Are you serious?"

He laughed. "Don't act so shocked. I think you have a great voice."

I stood with my arms out in amazement. "That's always been one of my dreams."

"Well, tomorrow night, then."

The next day I related my good news to Teresa. Just as I finished, an old family friend of hers walked into the bar. "Noah? How the heck are you?" She nearly jumped over the bar to embrace him. "Sue Ann, Noah and I go way back. He's a huge friend of my grandparents. In fact, he helped to raise me when I was younger."

Noah smiled. "Looks like she turned out alright,

though." He turned toward me. "Nice to meet you," he said with an extended hand.

"Yes, nice to meet you, too," I replied. *Handsome,* I thought and went back to work while Teresa and Noah caught up.

When Noah left, Teresa came over to me. "Now that's the guy you've got to be with. He's loaded, and he's getting a divorce."

"I could care less about the loaded part, and I'm not a particular fan of going through *his* divorce."

Teresa giggled. "Well, maybe he'll grow on you. He's coming back tonight to hear you sing. He's a musician himself, you know. He even has his own band."

I air-swatted her with the cloth I was using. "Teresa, what have you gotten me into?"

࿇࿇࿇

That night, the music manager handed me the mic. I was so nervous, I couldn't stand on the stage. I had to sit in the audience. I asked the band to play "Tennessee Waltz," my dad's favorite song. A hush fell over the room as I started to sing, and when I finished, I received a standing ovation. Noah made his way over to me afterward. "That was great, Sue Ann, really great!"

"Thanks, Noah. It was nice of you to come out."

"I think I am going to bring my friend John to hear you. Say, what do you think about coming with us to hear John play in Portland?"

"I think that would be fun, but my car headlights aren't working. They barely get me to work and back without going out on me."

"Well, you and I could ride together."

"Sure, that would be fun."

"How about Friday?"

"Friday's good."

❧❧❧

Friday was such a smashing success that Noah and I have been together ever since. After five years of dating, we quietly married in 1991. I accompanied his band in many of their performances as Noah played. In 1994, one of Noah's band members got an offer to go to Nashville. He invited the whole band to move with him and launch their careers.

"So what do you think about Nashville?" Noah asked me one night over dinner.

"I don't really think anything about Nashville," I replied coyly. "I do, however, think about Alaska."

"Alaska, eh?" Noah leaned back in his chair and scratched his beard. "I like it. I like it a lot."

Noah and I visited several times before finding a beautiful plot of land in the tiny community of Knik. We broke ground and built our home. Shortly after we moved in, we both looked at each other and said, almost in unison, "We need to find a church." Churches lined the main road all the way into town. We chose the one closest to us, Sunny Knik Chapel, and never left. It is the perfect blend of bluegrass roots and sound teaching. Noah plays bluegrass gospel music on the occasional Sunday, and I sing my heart out in the pews. Since we started attending in 1996, the congregation has grown to such an extent that seating in the sanctuary spills out into the foyer.

ॐॐॐ

"You have to stop waitressing." My doctor looked at me very seriously. "All good things must come to an end, and it's time for you to pick up another career or just enjoy your retirement."

"Doctor, I need something to keep me busy."

"Well, then, why don't you try going down to the MASST Center — I think it stands for Mature Alaskans Seeking Skills Training. They have part-time positions, and you may find something you like."

I went into town the next day and filled out an application. According to my interests, they placed me with an organization that sends homeless families with young children to churches willing to house them and provide them with hot meals. I started with them in June of 2010, and by December, I had convinced my boss to hire me permanently.

I praise God that he has brought me to a place where I can help people. I am amazed that God blessed me with a marriage that is based on love and trust, instead of alcohol and partying. And I love that God has established a legacy of reconciliation and having a relationship with Jesus in my family. I realize that God never promised that my life would be easy or fair, but he did promise to forgive me for the things I've done wrong and love me always. After 30 years of sobriety, I live my life like that old Christy Lane song, "One Day at a Time."

TO WAR AND BACK
The Story of Lynn Hoover
Written by Karen Koczwara

I held the razor blade to my wrist, my fingers trembling as the tip of it grazed my skin. With one deft move, I could end it all. I'd seen enough death to know how this worked. Within a few hours, I'd be lifeless and limp on the bottom of the shower floor, a pool of blood at my feet.

There would be no more pain, no more defeat, no more loneliness. I could forget the ugly monster I had become and the terrible, dark place I'd gotten myself into.

I could escape for good.

I took a deep breath and lowered the blade, ready to say goodbye to the cruel world.

But before I could make the first cut, something suddenly stopped me …

৵৵৵

I was born on August 15, 1950, in DuBois, Pennsylvania, a tiny rural town once known for its coal and lumber industry. When I was 5 years old, my father abruptly abandoned our family, leaving my mother to care for me and my two brothers by herself. We moved into my grandparents' little backwoods farmhouse and struggled to survive. The house included a coal furnace in the basement for heat, a wood-burning cook stove in the kitchen and an outhouse in the backyard. Because we had no running water, we had to haul our own from the nearby creek. The place was barely big enough to house us all, but we managed with what little we had.

Each morning, I made the quarter-mile trek to school down the road. It was a one-room red brick schoolhouse; one teacher taught all six grades. A wood-burning potbellied stove sat in the rear of the room to warm us during the chilly winter months.

My mother, depressed over our circumstances, began to drink. She had three more children out of wedlock, and soon she became the talk of our little town. I didn't understand much at my young age, but I knew that between my mother's troubles, our growing brood and our financial situation, we were in pretty bad shape.

Every few Sundays my mother took us to the little Baptist church in town. People stared as we walked through the doors — the poor, single, alcoholic mother with all those unruly boys.

"Isn't that the woman whose husband left her? I heard she drinks herself into a stupor all the time," a few folks whispered as we filed into the pews.

My cheeks flamed as I took my seat. I'd thought church people were supposed to be more loving, but instead they turned down their noses at us. When I was 8 years old, I told my mother I didn't want to go to church anymore. It hurt too bad to know people thought so poorly of us.

One morning, when I was 11, I went into my mother's room to wake her up. "C'mon, Mom, you slept in," I whispered, gently shaking her. But she didn't move. Growing frantic, I shook her some more, but her body was completely limp. Only then did I notice her pale lips and cheeks.

"Help! Help!" I raced out of the room and found my brother down the hall. "Mom's not waking up!" I cried.

We did not have a phone in the house. My brother ran down the road to the nearest neighbor's, and they called an ambulance. Terror mounted inside of me as the vehicle roared down the road, sirens blaring as it took my mother away. Later, I learned she had overdosed on sleeping pills in an attempt to kill herself. She could not take living in poverty and misery anymore.

Though my mother survived her suicide attempt, the State deemed her mentally unstable after the incident. She was placed in a mental institution and administered torturous shock therapy in an attempt to cure her. My mother was now not only known as the promiscuous town drunk, but also considered crazy and dangerous.

The social workers sent my brothers and me to live with different relatives. I went to my great aunt's house nearby. She was a nice Christian woman who held good values and tried to offer me a good home, but I was not receptive to her warmth. I was angry at myself for letting my mother down and felt I should have been able to protect her. I lashed out at everyone around me, and my behavior grew out of control.

At last, my great aunt could not tolerate me anymore. "You're going to live with your father in New York," she said. "Pack your things."

"My father?" I hadn't seen my father since I was 5. He had never once tried to reach out to me or my brothers. What would he be like after all these years? And would he want any sort of relationship with me?

New York, with its tall skyscrapers, blaring taxi cabs and bustling streets, was a stark change from the little rural town I'd grown up in. My heart beat quickly as my father approached me at the airport gate. I waited for him to scoop me up into a big hug and fire off a hundred questions, but instead he simply took my luggage and told me to get in the car.

When we pulled up at his house, I was shocked to see how nice it was. While my mother and I had been living in poverty, my father had been living in luxury — with a completely new family! He had a new wife, new kids and nicer toys than I'd ever seen in my life. There was even a shiny motorcycle in the garage — something I'd always dreamed of owning. I couldn't keep my jaw from dropping as I toured his beautiful home. He was a complete stranger to me, and I suddenly grew angry as I realized that he had been getting on just fine after turning his back on us. How could he do something like this?

I remained miserable in New York until my mother was released from the hospital six months later; I then returned to live with her. Though she tried her best to go on with life, she still struggled with addiction. I grew angry with the injustice of our circumstances. I still could not believe my father had the nerve to lead a completely different life in a different state while we barely survived on welfare. I felt abandoned by the world and was determined to get away from it all.

When I was 14, I tried to run away, but the cops quickly brought me back. I continued to make trouble at home and plotted how I could escape my miserable life. At 17, I hitchhiked to Ohio with a friend. My uncle worked in the oil fields there, and I hoped he might be able to hire us on. My friend and I had 17 cents between us as we crossed the state line.

When we arrived in Ohio, my uncle agreed to pay two weeks rent for my friend and me in the boardinghouse where he lived. He gave us $50 each and told us to go find a job.

"If something comes up at the oil field, I'll let you know right away," my uncle promised.

I found work as a telephone splicer's assistant. My uncle got promoted and hired on my friend, then hired me a few weeks later as a roughneck on an oil rig. We worked grueling 12- to 16-hour days alongside a bunch of guys who liked to drink, swear and complain about their miserable lives. After their shift was over, they hit the local bars and drank until they stumbled home and grabbed a few hours of sleep before getting up to do it all over again. As I watched their lifestyle, the insanity of it all hit me.

"This is crazy," I told my friend one night as I shook the dirt out of my boots and mopped the sweat from my brow. "I don't know about you, but I can't keep this up, working with no purpose."

I returned to Pennsylvania, and my friend and I soon got arrested for attempted robbery. When our case went to court, we encountered a friendly judge who had mercy on us.

"You guys are both young and have no serious crimes in your past. I'll give you one chance to keep your records clean. If you enlist in the military, I'll drop all your charges," the judge said kindly.

I agreed to enlist, and in September 1967, my mother signed the papers, releasing me to the United States Army. The military had received another troubled, angry young man.

I finished my Basic Training at Fort Jackson, South Carolina, and then went on to advanced infantry training at Fort Dix, New Jersey. Many of the military guys smoked marijuana, and when they offered me some, I didn't object. Though the smoke burned my lungs as it went down, I liked the mellow high that kicked in a few minutes later.

The Christmas season arrived, and I flew back home to Pennsylvania. When I arrived, however, I found the little farmhouse empty. After asking around town, I learned that my entire family had packed up and moved to Los Angeles, California, while I was away. They'd left no forwarding address; just like that, they were gone.

I found an aunt still in town, and she let me stay with her and her family during my leave. "I just can't understand how they could do something like that," I told her, shaking my head. "Why wouldn't they even call or just let me know where they were going?"

"I'm sorry, Lynn. It just all happened so quickly," she said with a sigh.

My friend called a couple of days before Christmas. "Hey, my brother let me borrow his '55 Chevy convertible," he said. "You wanna go out drinking with us?"

"Sure, why not?" I agreed. My family had abandoned me on one of the most important holidays of the year. Why would I turn down a party? I hopped in his car, and we sped off to grab a few drinks.

The next thing I knew, I was waking up in the back seat of the car. My entire body shook as I rubbed my eyes and tried to figure out where I was. What had just happened?

"Son, you've been in an accident," I heard a man say. "Just lay still there, okay?"

"Oh, man, and what an accident that was," another voice piped up.

An accident? Why couldn't I remember a thing? I racked my brain, trying to replay the events of the night. I had been with my buddies, pounding a few beers and attempting to drown my troubles. I vaguely remembered climbing back in his car to head home — what had happened between then and now?

The ride to the hospital felt like a fuzzy dream. A flurry of doctors and nurses attended to me when we arrived, checking my vitals and asking me questions. Machines buzzed and bleeped all around me, and what seemed like a million IVs and wires surrounded my bed. As I began to sober up, the searing pain set in. "Can someone tell me what happened?" I moaned.

"You were in a very bad car accident," a doctor informed me. "You hit a rock ledge going 70 miles per hour. To be honest, the only reason you and your friends are alive is because you were so drunk."

Rock ledge. Seventy miles per hour. Lucky to be alive. As I processed his words, the reality of it all sunk in. A fun night out with friends had nearly turned tragic; I could have been dead. But with my family living clear across the country now, would anyone have even noticed if I never made it back home?

I spent several weeks in the local hospital before being moved to the military hospital in Fort Dix to continue recovering. Slowly, I regained my strength, and at last I was released and completed my training at Fort Dix. Upon graduation, I went on to jump school at Fort Benning, Georgia, to become a paratrooper. From there, I was assigned to Fort Bragg, North Carolina, with the 82nd Airborne Division.

My evenings consisted of drinking and smoking pot. I was still angry with life, angry with my family and angry with the world. Pounding a few beers or smoking a joint or two was an easy way to distract myself from my troubles, and because everyone around me did it, also, it didn't seem like a big deal. I got in fights on a regular basis, trying to prove I was tougher than the rest of the guys. I didn't need any friends — I didn't need *anyone.*

Eventually, I tired of the strict policies in the 82nd Airborne Division. In 1968, I decided to go AWOL. I left for the West Coast and turned myself in at Ford Ord, California. I was immediately court-martialed and thrown in the Fort Ord stockade. It proved to be one of the most frightening experiences of my life.

The moment I arrived in the dingy stockade, I noticed many tough-looking, hardened men. The guys stared me down, their eyes steely and threatening as I shuffled to my bunk. Down the hall, I heard loud screams, curse words and slamming doors. The whole scene was worse than anything I had imagined or seen on TV. To protect myself from being attacked, I slid under the bunk and slept on the cold, hard floor for the next three days.

When my case was processed, the officers assigned me to one of three large 60-man cells. The moment they slammed the door behind me, a guy marched over and threatened me with obscenities.

"Well, I'll be the deadest piece you'll ever get because you're going to have to kill me first," I snarled. On impulse, I drop-kicked him in the chest, knocked him to the ground and shoved my boot in his face. Angrily, I kicked him repeatedly until the guards rushed in and yanked me off.

"We don't mess around in here like that, son," the guard hissed at me as he marched me down the hall. "You're getting solitary confinement for 10 days."

Though solitary confinement was terribly dark, lonely and boring, a small part of me was relieved to be away from the threats. After 10 long days, the guards threw me back in the cell. While I was gone, a little guy from Kentucky had been assigned to the cell.

"Look, man, you gotta just lay low around here. These guys are crazy," I whispered, trying to warn him before he got hurt.

But he didn't heed my words. Moments later, one of the guys swaggered up to him and stared him in the eye. "Shine my boots for me, kid," he ordered.

The kid from Kentucky shot back with a racial slur, and the other guys in the cell piped up one by one. "Yeah, we've had enough of this s***," they cried. "Leave us the h*** alone!"

Their bold retorts unleashed a war. That evening, the other guys met in the showers to discuss a plan. When they returned to the cell, they wielded homemade weapons and charged at us. My adrenaline kicked in as I stepped up to fight them off. I glanced back, expecting to see the other 30 guys in line to fight them as well, but only a handful remained. The rest huddled in the back of the cell, fearing for their lives.

I threw myself in the middle, ready for a good fight. I used every tactic I'd learned in the military, punching, hitting, kicking and throwing my opponents as they fought back. When at last the guards stepped in to intervene, I was a bloody mess on the ground. They carted all of us off to the hospital, treated our injuries and returned us to minimum custody in the stockade the next day.

That night, as we stood in line for chow, a few of the guys who had attacked us suddenly stepped out of line, jumped and stabbed the poor guy from Kentucky. I watched in horror as blood spurted out of his gut, and he crumpled to the ground just feet away. He died from a ruptured spleen that night.

The next night, one of the guys who had stood with me in the riot was so frightened that he decided to escape the stockade. He managed to sneak out of the cell and was halfway over the fence when he was shot and killed. When I learned the news, I felt sick to my stomach. I had heard many stories about military prisons since enlisting, but I'd had no idea things were this horrific behind those barbed wires. I wasn't sure how much longer I could go on, fearing for my life every night as I slept and trying to keep from getting jumped when I turned my back. I knew I'd have to be alert at every moment and just hope I made it out alive.

I managed to survive the rest of my incarceration without further incident, and I breathed a heavy sigh of relief when I walked out that cell door for the last time. The military assigned me to an administrative position in Fort Ord. I served there for a year before receiving orders to ship out to Vietnam. I was going to war, but I felt like I had already lived through one in that terrifying prison.

On September 9, 1969, I arrived in Vietnam and was assigned to an airborne brigade as an infantryman in a combat platoon. My platoon sent a squad in to pick me up and take me back to base with them. We stopped at a small village to eat a quick evening meal along the way. Our medic had just finished his meal and was washing his hands at a nearby well. I had heard he was a respectable, compassionate guy, but he quickly proved me wrong.

He marched over to his rucksack and came running back a few moments later. "Alright, who stole my cigarettes and my lighter?" he screamed.

I stood there, my feet frozen to the ground. The medic charged toward our interpreter and threatened, "Tell the village people to return my stuff, or I'm gonna burn this village down, understand?"

The interpreter nodded, his eyes wide with fear. He rushed off to tell the village people what the medic had said, but no one came forward with his cigarettes. The medic grew angrier, his eyes fiery with rage as he grabbed another lighter and lit a handful of straw on fire. He then raced up and down the path, waving the fiery straw in the air and lighting the huts on fire one by one. I watched in horror as the flames leapt into the air. Was this guy crazy? Why was he trying to burn the whole village down over a pack of cigarettes?

Half of the little village was on fire by the time military officials stepped in to stop him. I stood to the side as thick black smoke curled into the air. I was just a 19-year-old kid, halfway across the world from home, and I had just officially stepped into a war zone. *Welcome to Vietnam,* I thought with disgust as I headed back to my base.

I helped run patrols in the area for the next several weeks. One day, as we prepared to go out into the bush, our officers ordered us to line up our equipment and wait for the choppers to arrive. I had just taken a seat on the steps of a supply room when a guy sidled up to me and said he wanted to sit down.

"Here, have a seat," I offered, scooting over.

He glared at me. "No, get up. I want to sit there," he barked.

"I said there's plenty of room. Have a seat," I repeated, forcing a smile.

The guy turned on the heels of his boots, marched over to his equipment and picked up his M-16 rifle. He loaded it, put a round in the chamber and stormed back over to me. "I said move," he ordered, pointing the rifle in my face.

I stared him straight in the eyes. "F*** you!" I hissed.

Out of nowhere, three guys raced forward and jumped him. They wrestled him to the ground, grabbed the weapon out of his arms and dragged him away. I sat there, my heart thudding in my chest as I tried to regain my composure. I knew I couldn't win with guys like that. I could only hope that they'd leave me alone so one of us didn't end up eventually killing the other.

Our platoon was sent to Ash Shaw Valley, which was known for high concentrations of enemy traps and booby traps. While we were out patrolling the highways one evening, a firefight ensued on our base, and the platoon sergeant and the radio operator ran for cover in opposite directions. In doing so, they ripped the handset off the radio and lost all communications. When we returned, they assumed we were enemy attackers and began shooting us as we got close.

When at last we cleared up the confusion, the half of our platoon that had remained on base told us to go find the other half of our platoon that had dispersed to go after their attackers. They explained that we should head toward the railroad tracks that ran through the valley and call them when we arrived to receive further instructions.

We did as we were told, and as we neared the tracks, one of the platoon members back at base called. "Stop right there," he warned. "Someone will come down and guide you where to go next."

In Vietnam, we knew that one wrong move, too soon or too late, could cost us our lives. While on foot patrol, I whipped around to check behind us when all of a sudden, everything exploded into a ball of flames before my eyes. The force of the explosion picked me up and threw me several feet, and I landed hard on my back. Instantly, pain shot through my body, and I knew I was badly hurt. I was alive, though — but had the others in my platoon survived the blast?

I spent the next two weeks in a hospital in Qui Nhon, recovering from my wounds. As I lay there wrapped in thick bandages, I mourned the other guys who hadn't been so lucky. The blast had instantly wiped out a seven-man squad. The other five guys were sent to hospitals in Japan and the United States. And as for the new guy who'd just joined our platoon, the only thing left of him was his left foot and his ID card. A young man with all the promise of tomorrow, he would never return to his family again.

The reality of the deaths and my own fortunate escape hit me as I lay in that hospital bed. I had known there would be death; I had known it might be gruesome. But I knew those faces by name. I'd heard their laughs and knew their stories. I knew where they came from. And now they were gone, just like that. A piece of my heart hardened as I realized this was just the beginning. There would be more loss, and those death toll numbers could include me.

ॐॐॐ

I finished my tour without further injuries and was discharged back to the United States. I returned to Pennsylvania and found work in a foundry, a factory that produced metal castings. The factory was obsolete and deadly; most men who retired from working there died six months later from black lung. But I needed a job and quickly found I was good at it. I got promoted to running an electric ladle full of hot metal, pouring it into molds. The work was tedious but passed quickly.

One hot August afternoon, I got careless and decided not to put on my thick heavy apron that protected me from the neck to the knees. As I started to pour an eight-inch mold, an air bubble popped through the seam of the mold, spattering scalding hot molten all over me. It instantly burned through my clothing and onto my chest, legs and private parts. I screamed out in pain and immediately ran to the doctor. Two days later, I quit my job.

After recovering from the burns, I approached the Army recruiter and told him I wanted to re-enlist. As horrific as the military life could be, it was also what I knew best. After only nine months of civilian life, I was on a plane back to Vietnam.

Upon learning my old unit was being sent back to the United States, I showed up at a meeting with the Charlie 75th Rangers. A stocky man named Captain Slaughter lumbered to the front of the room and stared out at us, his eyes hard and unflinching.

"Gentlemen, the first thing I have to tell you is that we have a 50 percent loss ratio in our unit. That means that if all of you join our unit, half of you are already dead!" he announced coldly.

I stared back at him and shrugged. *Maybe I'll be one of the 50 percent who make it,* I thought half-heartedly. *And maybe not.* The military life, coupled with a tumultuous childhood, had hardened me, and some days I didn't care much if I lived or died. There was nothing left for me back in the United States. What did I have to lose?

After six months, my unit disbanded and prepared to return to the United States. When I arrived for processing at Brigade Headquarters in Pleiku, I approached the desk of the first sergeant. I was fully de-humanized by now. I sported a full beard, a Mohawk haircut and a necklace made of a human ear around my neck. When the sergeant took a look at me, he jumped up and ran around the desk like a mad man.

"What Army do you think you are in, and what's that s*** on your face?" he barked. "Where are you being assigned?"

When I told him, he lashed out again. "That's my unit. You better watch your back, kid," he snarled, his eyes growing to slits as he stared me down.

I was assigned to a security platoon with another ranger; our job was to protect the bunker line on the compound at Camp Holloway, just a few miles outside Pleiku. I soon learned that all the guys assigned to this particular platoon were heroin addicts. After I'd been there a few weeks, the compound was sealed off for three days in an attempt to catch all the junkies who ran out of their smack.

During this time, I came down with a terrible fever and began vomiting profusely. When I became pale and lethargic, the officers in command admitted me to the local hospital. As I lay there writhing in bed, the first sergeant stopped by just as the doctor made his rounds.

"I'm glad you finally busted this junkie ranger," the sergeant gloated. "Serves him right."

"What are you talking about? This young man has a serious case of malaria," the doctor informed him, checking his chart.

"No, that's not right. I know a junkie when I see one, and this guy has all the signs!"

The first sergeant proceeded to argue with the doctor at the foot of my bed as I lay there, too weak and tired to defend myself.

"I can show you the test results, if you like," the doctor replied calmly. "This is classic malaria, not withdrawal symptoms."

I knew the first sergeant had had it out for me since our first meeting and had been looking for any reason to bust me. His assumptions about my character were based purely on my rough-looking appearance, and this angered me. I was happy when his tour ended and he rotated back to the United States.

But it wasn't long before I began snorting heroin along with my fellow rangers. I didn't care about anything anymore. If those in charge already thought I was trouble, why try to stay away from it?

A new young lieutenant was assigned as leader of our security platoon. He showed up on a Saturday with 10 cases of beer and introduced himself.

"Let's have a little party to get to know one another," he suggested.

The day before, one of the men in our platoon had gotten a package of downer pills called "reds" in the mail. We began mixing booze and downers, which proved to be a terrible mistake. By 1 p.m., the whole platoon was so wasted they began to fight with each other, cursing and pushing as they wandered around in a stupor.

"Gentlemen, get into formation! The party's over!" the lieutenant ordered, stepping into the middle of the chaos.

"You need to sleep this off so you can report for duty tonight!"

We stumbled over each other, but we were too strung out to get into formation. At last, the first sergeant arrived on the scene to intervene.

"Gentlemen! The party's over! Everyone get to bed!" he screamed.

I finished my tour of duty in Vietnam and returned to the States. I managed to get off the heroin, but I kept drinking and doing every other drug I could get my hands on. I knew I had post traumatic stress disorder (PTSD), something everyone in the military said was common after enduring such horrific conditions. I was completely lost, lonely and full of rage, just waiting to go off on anyone who got in my path.

I got reassigned to Fort Bragg, North Carolina, but got fed up with my division and went AWOL again. I turned myself in at Fort Ord, California, reconnected with my mother and family and eventually got a job as a clerk in a Basic Training company there. I spent the next three years there and continued to drink and abuse drugs. I met a woman at Fort Ord, and we got married. Shortly after, I got promoted to sergeant and received orders for Fort Richardson, Alaska.

I was anxious for a change of scenery and pace. My wife had children from a previous marriage, and at first we all seemed to get along. But the more I struggled with my addictions, the worse the tension in our home became.

"You've gotta get control of yourself, Lynn," my wife

screamed at me one night after I flew into a rage. "You're seriously starting to scare me, you know that?"

"Just shut up, and leave me the h*** alone!" I hurled back. No one had prepared me for this marriage thing. My parents had both struggled with their own demons, and their marriage had been an ultimate failure. I had never known the meaning of true love; I had only hoped that by getting married, some of the pain I'd buried beneath the mask of my hardened appearance would be eased by finding a wife of my own. But the pain only doubled the more we lashed out at each other.

One night, as I lay in bed after drinking too much, I began to fantasize about taking out my wife and any other person who got close to me. I envisioned myself killing them all and dumping their bodies in a bloody mess on the ground. The more I tossed and turned, the worse my thoughts grew. I decided that if I did not get away from everyone soon, I would follow through with these horrific acts in real life.

"I can't stay with you anymore," I told my wife one day. "If I don't leave, something bad is going to happen." And just as my father had up and left our family, I did the same to mine. I told myself I was protecting them, doing them a favor by fleeing. I went AWOL again, this time for four months. When I finally returned to my old unit in Alaska, I learned my wife had returned to California.

Before I was thrown back in the stockade, I informed those in charge, "I'm here to be processed for discharge. I'm ready to get out of the Army for good."

TO WAR AND BACK

I received my discharge on December 13, 1976 and was released onto the streets of Anchorage, Alaska. As I stood there on a street corner downtown, the winter chill whipping at my cheeks, I felt completely lost. I glanced around at the stores with their bright lights, the cars honking their horns and the families shuffling briskly down the sidewalks. I felt like a 5-year-old kid on a street corner in New York City, completely clueless as to where to go or who to ask for help. I reached deep inside and tried to muster some sort of emotion, but I came up empty. The harsh military life had left me hardened, without an ounce of compassion in my heart. I was a walking dead man, a nobody to the world. And if I hadn't been so numb, the very idea of it all would have sent me to my knees in heaving sobs.

かかか

I called up some old friends and asked if I could stay with them for a bit while I got on my feet. With no direction or purpose, I started dealing drugs to support myself and my habit. The money was good, but I knew this wasn't how I wanted to make a living.

For the first time in my life, I started searching for something. I hadn't a clue what it was, but somewhere deep in my gut, I knew there was more to life than just existing. I picked up a few books at the library on astral projection and metaphysics and flipped through them, desperate to discover some deeper meaning to life.

Suddenly, I was yearning for the truth, whatever the truth might be.

My mother called one day. "Your wife has officially divorced you," she informed me. "I guess you're free to get on with your life."

A mixture of sadness and relief filled my heart. I had loved my wife, but I'd known from the start that I could never be what she wanted me to be in my wrecked state of mind.

I met another woman a few months later, and we began dating. She had a 4-year-old son. With big eyes and a charming smile, he instantly melted my heart. We played hide and seek, drew pictures together and tossed the ball in the yard. I loved the way he accepted me so easily, and I did the same with him. There was no pretense between us, no heavy expectations, just an easy, comfortable love. It was a beautiful thing.

I started reading a book called *Taking Yourself Apart and Putting Yourself Back Together Again.* My eyes fell onto a particular question that struck me: "How does the world see you?" I thought about it for a moment. I had started running from the pain so early on in my life, I'd never stopped to look at what I was becoming or how anyone saw me.

As I stood in the shower that night, the hot water running down my back, I closed my eyes and asked myself again, "How does the world see me?" At that very moment, a movie of my life played backward in my mind, and I slowly saw every horrible, ugly, hateful thing I'd ever done. How had I gotten to this place? I certainly hadn't woken up one morning and decided to be a drug addict, a killer or a drunk.

Tears spilled down my cheeks, mixing with the shower water, and I spoke to God for the very first time. "If you are real, God, if you exist, talk to me!" I cried out. "I would rather be dead than be what I've become!"

At my wit's end, I grabbed my razor blade and held it to my wrist, ready to put my pain to rest for good. But just before the blade sliced through my skin, I heard the very real voice of a very real God clearly in my mind. In my desperate moment, he stepped into that shower with me, wrapped his loving arms around me and spoke to my heart.

I immediately fell to my knees and started weeping. Right then and there in the shower, I prayed, "God, please come into my heart. I know that you are what I've been searching for my whole life. You are the only one who can fill the empty hole in my heart. I need you to restore me and forgive the wrong things I've done. Thank you for loving me just as I am."

As I stood back up and shut the water off, an indescribable peace overcame me, and I felt lighter from head to toe. I stared at the razor on the ground, unable to believe I had almost sliced my wrists with it. There was no way to make sense of what had just happened — it was simply God. He had put words in my heart, and as he spoke them to me, the hardened heart I'd held onto for so long simply melted away. Suddenly, nothing else made sense. There was no drug, no drink, no girlfriend, no library book that could take my pain away. There was only God.

As I went to bed that night, I felt hope for the first time in years. I thought back to the few times I'd attended church as a young boy. I remembered the pastor sharing that God wanted to invite all of us into a relationship with him and that we only needed to ask forgiveness for the wrong things we'd done and accept his love. It had seemed so simple and almost too good to be true, especially for a boy who felt unloved at home. But I now realized that it really was that simple. There were no gimmicks, no strings attached. I did not need to come up with fancy words to impress God; I simply had to give him my heart.

I had spent most of my life as an angry young man, but I did not want to live that way any longer. I knew that I needed to escape from my current drug lifestyle, but I didn't know how to do it. I didn't know any other Christians in the area or even own a Bible. But I prayed often, talking to God as though he was my new best friend. Whenever I felt alone or confused, I turned to him first instead of trying to do things on my own.

But I continued to struggle with addiction. My girlfriend grew concerned. "I think you really need help, Lynn," she urged me. She abused drugs as well, but she seemed to think I was more messed up.

"I'm trying to get clean," I promised. I told her about God and how he had spoken to me in the shower and how something had radically changed in my heart. I so badly wanted to leave behind my old lifestyle for good, but I was simply in too deep.

My girlfriend and I got married and had two sons together. I got a job and slowly started to make better choices for our family. But my addiction continued to plague me.

One night, I came home from work to find my wife in bed with our coke dealer. I flew into a rage. "How could you do this to me?" I screamed.

"I'm sorry, Lynn," she whimpered. "But I want a divorce."

"I'll save you the trouble," I snarled. I shoved a pistol in my pocket and peeled out of the driveway in my work van. A few miles down the road, I pulled over, parked and cried out to God. "You told me love was the answer, God! Well, if this is love, I would rather be dead!"

I put the barrel of the gun in my mouth and cocked the trigger. Just as I was about to pull it, God spoke to my heart as he had in the shower that night.

And just like that, the anxiousness that had filled my heart moments earlier was replaced with an unexplainable peace. I put down the gun, drove home and told my wife that God had given me peace. "You are free to do whatever you want to do," I told her calmly.

My wife filed for divorce shortly after, and I continued to struggle with drugs and drinking. I secured a Bible and began to read it eagerly, trying to absorb as much as I could. But in my mind, a different voice, full of contempt, tried to discourage me with painful thoughts of my childhood as I remembered the church that had snubbed me and my family. I wanted to find a church and reach out to other Christians, but what if they rejected me because of my past?

One night, as I read my Bible, a certain phrase we'd used in the Rangers came back to me: "Death before dishonor, and never surrender!" *Surrender.* I thought about the word for a moment. It meant giving up yourself to another being, letting go of everything. Suddenly, I realized that's just what I had to do. I had to completely surrender my life, the ugly parts and all, to God and trust that he would work it all out.

I left Alaska and went to California to visit my family and do some soul searching. I hated being away from my children, but I knew it was the right thing to do. My mother and I had a great conversation during our visit, and I thanked God for restoring our relationship. I now understood that she was a victim of life's difficult circumstances and that she had tried the very best that she could as a parent.

I struggled with loneliness while I was away, and again, God answered me with comforting words in the form of a poem. The words permeated my heart, and I thanked him for comforting me. Despite the struggles I still faced, I knew that he was working in me, drawing me to him with his unconditional love. He was so patient, so kind. He knew I was a work in progress, yet he did not give up on me, and I was grateful for that.

After several months, I returned to Alaska and moved

to the Mat-Su Valley, where I found a place to live. My two sons lived with me on and off for the next several years, and I tried to be the best father I could. But I still had an uncontrollable rage that reared its ugly head from time to time, and it frightened me. I knew I needed help for my post traumatic stress disorder; it was time to take the step and reach out.

I found a doctor in Anchorage who specialized in PTSD and decided to visit him. As I pulled into the parking garage for my first visit, my chest tightened, my hands began to tingle, I had trouble breathing and my arms became completely paralyzed on the steering wheel. I sat there for several minutes until I could compose myself.

"You were having a panic attack," the doctor explained when I told him what had happened. "It's very common with PTSD. I'm going to prescribe you some medication to help with the anxiety." He went on to describe that while there was no real cure for the disorder, it was important to understand what it was and why I reacted the way I did.

I felt hopeful as my treatment began. I settled in the little town of Knik, Alaska, in 1989 and tried to get my life in order. But I still could not let go of the drugs. In 1995, I got busted for growing pot and received five years of probation.

At this point, I realized that I needed to completely surrender my life to God. I had given him portions of my life since inviting him into my heart, but I had never fully surrendered everything.

"God, I know I can't do this on my own," I prayed, desperate to change for good. "But I know that Philippians 4:13 (KJV) says that 'I can do all things through Christ who strengthens me.' Help me to do the right things and live for you. I trust you with my whole heart."

The following year, my mother called with surprising news. "Your father and his wife are coming to Alaska to visit. They want to see you."

I gulped hard. I had forgiven my father for abandoning me as a child, but would I be able to truly reach out to him in person?

With God's strength, I was able to show my father love when he and his wife arrived for a 10-day visit. I knew it must be God at work in my heart, because I felt at peace the entire time they were there. When they left, I thanked God for helping me to extend unconditional love.

Though I continued to pray and read my Bible, I knew there was still one more thing I had to do. I needed to reach out to a church.

I was still afraid people might judge me for my past, but it was time to set aside my fears and trust that God would place me just where he wanted me to be. It was time to take that next brave step.

❧❧❧

"I'm so glad to hear you've given your heart to God," I told the prisoner as I stood to leave. "It's never too late to start a relationship with him. I'll be praying for you."

As I drove home, I thanked God for the miracle I'd just seen. Since getting involved with the prison ministry several years earlier, I'd watched many once-hardened men surrender their hearts to God. They reminded me a bit of the man I'd once been — tough-looking on the outside and callous on the inside. But God had given me a new heart, and slowly those rough edges had disappeared. The man I'd just spoken with was serving a life sentence for murder, but as I shared God's love with him, he, too, found hope for the first time in his life. Because of his decision, he could face life in prison while trusting that when he died, he would spend eternity with God in heaven.

I'd gotten involved at Sunny Knik Chapel in Wasilla, and the church people were now more than friends — they were family. After I took the step to reach out to others, they had reached right back out to me with open arms. For the first time in my life, I experienced what it was like to be surrounded by people who loved me just as I was.

One day, I asked Pastor Duane what it meant to really live out the Christian life. His answer was simple. "It's learning to be self-sacrificial instead of self-centered. After all, that's what Jesus did for us."

His words pierced my heart. Along with the prison ministry, I decided to get involved with the food bank and began driving the church van. It was a privilege to serve others and show them the unconditional love God had extended to me.

The angry man with the Mohawk was now gone, along with any urge for drugs or alcohol. In his place was a man filled with hope, love, peace and joy. I had indeed been to war and back, but I was no longer a prisoner of pain. I had truly been set free.

RELENTLESS LOVE
The Story of Teri Johnson
Written by Karen Koczwara

"What are you doing? Are you trying to kill me?!" I screamed as the bullet ricocheted off the floor and hit the TV. The screen shattered and turned to static as I dove in the corner for cover.

My husband turned angrily to me, his eyes fiery as he pressed the gun between his palms. "Why don't you just shut up, Teri?" he threatened in a steely voice.

I tried to keep my voice steady as I hunched on my heels. "I'll do whatever you say," I offered, attempting a pleasant tone. I put my hands behind my back so he would not see them trembling.

"Whatever." My husband stormed off, twirling the gun in his fingers like a plastic toy.

I drew a deep breath of relief and tried to regain my composure. This wasn't the first time he'd gotten so angry, but it was the first time I thought he might actually try to kill me. I knew I could not go on like this, living in fear in my own home. I would have to choose to leave, even if it meant losing everything.

☙☙☙

I was born in Inglewood, California, in 1953, the second child to two hardworking middle-class parents. My older brother and I were close, and when my younger sister arrived, we included her in our fun. We moved east to the city of Rialto just as I entered school, and I joined the Girl Scouts in third grade. The program became the highlight of my life. I loved learning campfire songs, making special craft projects, meeting new friends and exploring the great outdoors.

I was close with my grandmother, who went with us to church on Easter, Christmas and other holidays. I didn't understand much about the message, but I sure liked the songs. They reminded me a bit of the ones we sang in Girl Scouts — happy and upbeat. I looked forward to the sixth grade at school, when I could be in the Christmas program and sing on the stage.

But just before the sixth grade, my father announced his work was transferring him to Alaska; our family would be moving.

We took a helicopter from San Bernardino to the Los Angeles airport, where we prepared to board another plane headed north. As we flew over the rows of little houses with the backyard swimming pools and cement block fences, tears streamed down my cheeks. I didn't want to move away; I liked my life in Southern California just the way it was.

"I know this seems hard right now, but it will all be okay. You'll see," my mother said gently, pulling me in for a hug.

Alaska, with its rugged terrain, endless miles of greenery, abundant wildlife and clear blue skies, was a far cry from crowded, smoggy Southern California. My mother got pregnant and gave birth to another little girl that year, but not long after my sister arrived, my father quit his job. We returned to California and moved back into the same house, and life resumed its pace. I returned to Girl Scouts, focused on school and soon made new friends.

As I entered high school, I noticed my parents' marriage start to crumble. My father had never had a father in his life, and he struggled with relationships. He and my mother slept in separate rooms, and the fighting between them grew more and more terrible. I tried to get close to my father, but he often brushed me off as nothing but a dumb girl.

When I was 16, I joined the Model A Ford Club and learned how to work on cars. I offered to help my father as he tinkered with our own car in the garage, but he always put me down.

"You're not doing it right. Here, give me that wrench. Forget it, Teri. Just go back inside," my father snapped, slamming the hood of the car.

I sighed. It seemed I could do nothing right in his eyes.

My senior year, I took a food service class at school. I enjoyed learning about the food industry and wondered if I might be able to find a job at the local McDonald's. I stopped in one day to speak with the manager and noticed only men working there. They all wore crisp black pants, white shirts and ties.

"Don't you hire girls?" I asked the manager.

"Well, we've never really had any girls interested in working here before," he replied, looking a bit puzzled.

"I'm interested," I piped up. "How do I apply?"

The manager finally agreed to give me a chance, and he ordered me a gold smock uniform to wear. I felt like a pioneer woman, forging the way for other girls who wanted a chance to work in fast food. I loved flipping hamburgers and serving happy customers, and the nice little paycheck was an added bonus, too. I met a guy at work, and we began dating. He was charming and sweet, and within no time, I fell hard for him.

In 1971, my brother began attending church regularly. He invited me to the youth group, and I reluctantly agreed to go. I was a shy girl and had difficulty talking to people I didn't know well. Although the people were friendly enough, after a few visits, I quit going.

"There's really something to this stuff," my brother told me excitedly. "I want you to know that I invited Jesus into my life. I've been reading the Bible a lot, and it's all really making sense. I now understand that knowing Jesus isn't just about going to church on Sunday or hanging out with good people, but about really having a relationship with him in my heart."

"That's cool," I told him casually. I enjoyed the music and the social aspect of church, but I wasn't convinced that I needed God in my life. I seemed to be doing just fine without him.

In early September, my brother and his fiancée took a road trip back to Washington, D.C. to visit friends. My brother was excited to DJ an event with his buddy when he arrived. On their way back to California, he and his fiancée hit a storm in Arizona, and when a horse ran into their path, they crashed their car; he was instantly killed. His fiancée, who had switched seats with him just minutes before, survived the accident.

Our family reeled at the loss. I took it especially hard, as we had been so close. His words eerily echoed in my mind. "I'll probably die in a car someday, but I promise that I won't take anyone with me," the car enthusiast had once told my mother. And now he was gone too soon, leaving behind a girl he'd never marry and dreams he'd never fulfill. Our hearts were all broken.

I married my boyfriend on June 24, 1972. Almost immediately our home turned tumultuous as the honeymoon period wore off and my new husband grew abusive.

"Why can't you clean up this d*** kitchen?" my husband screamed at me one day after work. He picked up a dirty plate and threw it against the wall. I watched in horror as it shattered into tiny pieces on the countertop.

"What are you doing?" I cried. "Stop it!"

"Then stop making such a d*** mess around here," he snarled, picking up another plate.

"Stop it! Just stop it!" I raised my voice to match his and tried to grab the plate out of his hands. But he pushed me away and threw it at the wall. I stormed out of the kitchen in tears, too upset to clean up the mess.

In 1974 we welcomed a daughter into our home. That

same year, my parents separated, and my mother got a job offer to open up a bank in Mammoth.

Two years later, I gave birth to our son, and my husband got laid off from his job at the steel mill. We decided to move to Mammoth, too. I had always loved the mountains and lakes and secretly hoped to live by a Girl Scout camp someday. But a year later my husband returned to work at the steel mill, and we returned to Southern California, this time to the rural city of Hesperia. I hoped our marriage would improve, but instead it only grew worse.

One Thanksgiving morning, I crawled around the floor with my daughter, playing and laughing with her. When I got up, my husband stood there, glaring at my feet.

"You aren't going to wear those shoes to my mother's now, are you?" he asked, frowning.

I glanced down. "What's wrong with them?"

"You rubbed the suede off when you were crawling around down there. Now look at them. You can't wear those shoes, Teri."

I was shocked he had noticed such a tiny detail. "Um, okaaaay," I stammered. As I stomped off to change my shoes, I grew angry inside. Just as I could do nothing right in my father's eyes, I could do nothing right for my husband, either. A slightly messy house, a dirty dish or an object out of place warranted outrage. How could I ever live up to his expectations?

"If you ever try to leave me, I'll take those kids from

you, and you'll never see them again," my husband often threatened me. "I'll always be able to provide more for them because I have a better job than you will ever be able to get."

I believed his words, and deep down, I hoped he might one day change and go back to being the fun-loving guy I'd married.

But his abusive ways continued. One evening, unable to take it anymore, I locked myself in the bathroom and began tearing wildly at my hair, hitting myself and crying. "I can't do this anymore!" I screamed at the mirror. "I can't fix it and make it better!" I continued to sob until the reflection staring back at me was a puffy-eyed, raging monster.

Suddenly, I heard an unmistakable voice in my head. "You have to stop this now, Teri, or you are going to cross a line and not come back."

I stopped my screaming and glanced around the room, but there was nobody there. I was sure I had heard the voice, though, clear as if someone had been standing next to me. But where had it come from, and what did it mean?

My husband and I owned guns and often went out shooting for fun. One evening he grew angry for no reason, grabbed his gun and shot at the living room floor. The bullet ricocheted and blew out the TV nearby. I ducked in the corner, afraid he might turn the gun on me next. Something in me snapped, and I realized I could not go on living this way.

Maybe one day when we go out shooting, there could

be an accident, and he could disappear, I thought to myself. The thought both horrified and relieved me. I had officially become terrorized by an abusive husband. It was time to pack my bags and leave.

I left my husband, took the kids and moved back to Mammoth, where I moved in with my mother. I got a job at the Shell gas station, and my friend offered to babysit the kids while I worked. My mother supported my decision to leave and helped me as much as she could. I was relieved to be away from my husband and proud of myself for mustering the courage to leave.

A guy I worked with made Christian music videos. He showed me a few of them and asked me what I thought. I wasn't very interested in God or church; it seemed everyone I knew who went to church was a hypocrite. I had always believed there was a God; back in Girl Scouts when I'd attended camp, I loved sitting out in nature during our quiet times. There was something bigger than me out there, I knew that much, but I wasn't so sure I'd find it at church.

Still, to appease my mother, I attended the big Lutheran church in town on Christmas Eve and other holidays. It didn't mean much to me, but I enjoyed the songs well enough, and the kids seemed to like going, too. But everyone around me still seemed fake. *I'm a nicer person than they are,* I told myself.

I got a job at a hospital, secured my own place and joined the local Search and Rescue team. One day, my husband called and asked if he could come visit the kids. I agreed to his visit; deep down, a part of me still hoped he might change so we could reconcile.

But shortly after arriving, he was back to his old ways. "What do you mean you joined Search and Rescue, Teri?" he barked at me. "You better not go out and kill yourself and leave those kids without a mother!"

"What are you talking about?" I retorted. "Why would I do that?"

But he ignored me, grabbed the phone and ripped it off of the wall. Horrified, I ran out of the room and used another phone to call the cops. They came and escorted him out of town. *Good riddance,* I thought as I watched him drive away. *Now I can go on with my life.*

That night, not long after he left, I heard a voice beneath the floorboards of my house. The house had been built on a hill; was it possible somebody was beneath it? Terror crept into my veins as I soon realized the voice belonged to my husband. Despite the message that he was not welcome around here anymore, he'd had the nerve to return.

"Get out of here, or I'll call the cops again!" I yelled at him through the floorboards. "And I mean it!"

I was at my wit's end with my husband. I picked up every self-help book I could find and thumbed through them, trying to figure out how to make my life better. I even dabbled with psychics and astrology, hoping I might find the answers within the stars. But nothing seemed to help, and I grew more miserable and confused than ever.

My mother moved back to the San Bernardino area. I

had obtained an EMT certification and learned that a hospital in her area had a program that trained Radiologic Technologists. I enjoyed working in the medical field and decided it would be a perfect opportunity to further my career. I got accepted into the program and relocated back to Southern California, moved in with my father and signed up for college classes. I wanted to support my children on my income so that I could prove to my husband and everyone else that I could make it on my own.

My mother began attending a new church, and I noticed her demeanor change. The congregation was very legalistic, and suddenly it seemed we could not eat anything, say anything or do anything because "God disapproved." I was already skeptical about the church, but her strange behavior made me even more leery. Was God just a dictator up in the sky who enjoyed making up a bunch of rules so we couldn't have any fun? That didn't seem very appealing to me.

"We don't celebrate Christmas or our birthdays anymore," my mother told me one day. "My birthday is the day I got baptized at the church."

"Mom, do you hear the way you sound?" I confronted her one day. "It sounds a little crazy, don't you think? You never used to think all this stuff was bad."

"Well, I do now," she said, defending herself. "And I'm very concerned for you, Teri. I don't want you to go to hell."

"Mom, please stop talking like that. You're scaring

me," I pleaded with her. *Surely, something is wrong with this picture,* I told myself. *Surely, if there is a God, he can't be anything like this.*

I continued to challenge my mother at every turn. When I made fudge one Christmas, I refused to give her some. "It's *Christmas* fudge," I said spitefully.

"Oh, now, Teri, that's enough!" my mother cried.

"Well, seriously, Mom, listen to yourself. All this talk about hell and how God doesn't want us to do this or that. How do you know the Bible was even written by God, anyway? Maybe it was written by Satan!"

My mother gasped at my last comment and marched out of the room. I stared after her, satisfied that I'd had the last word. Whatever this religious stuff was, I didn't want any of it.

I graduated from San Bernardino County Medical Center and the college in nearby Yucaipa with my associate's degree. I whizzed through every test and assignment, became class president and graduated with honors. It felt good to receive such recognition. I was 32 years old with my whole life ahead of me. Now was the time to decide what I really wanted to do.

I got an X-ray tech job back at the hospital in Mammoth, but I didn't stay long. Owning a house was now my top priority; I didn't want to raise my kids in rented condos or apartments for the rest of our lives. Because Mammoth was a resort area, the home prices were too expensive, so I began looking in magazines for other places to move. As I flipped through one, Jackson

Hole, Wyoming, caught my eye. Another resort town, it looked gorgeous, but I knew it was out of my price range.

A job opened up in Palmer, Alaska, and I decided to apply. I had enjoyed living there for a short time as a child, and it certainly had the mountains and lakes that I loved. When the hospital called to check my references, I decided I'd better go up and check it out before I committed to making such a big move.

I arrived in Homer, Alaska, in April of 1991. It was not the most beautiful time of year; spring would not arrive there for another month. But as the waves crashed against the beach and eagles soared over the shining water, the sight was truly breathtaking. After the Alaskan pipeline had been built, there was no work left for many laborers. They fled their homes, leaving the keys on the counter as they sought work elsewhere. House prices were at an all-time low, and I knew I could easily afford one. But I was still uncertain in my heart.

I slept in my car on the beach that first night because I could not afford a motel. The next morning, I made my way up to the Palmer area. Immediately upon arriving, I saw a street sign ahead; it read Teri Lou. My heart skipped a beat — Teri Lou was my full name! Was it meant to be?

As it began getting dark, I knew I needed to return to Anchorage for my flight home. I was still wrestling in my mind when a giant eagle swooped down in front of my car. I had fallen in love with eagles as a child after seeing them at the San Diego Zoo. I burst into tears at the sight, and suddenly a peace filled my heart.

I have to be here, I decided. *This is where I'm meant to move.*

I took the job in the radiology department at the hospital in Palmer and moved the children up. My husband finally gave up the fight and let me go. We had become more cordial in the years since I'd decided to move on with my life. I knew Alaska would be starkly different than the busy Southern California lifestyle, but I was eager for a fresh start.

I met a man named Sam, who repaired the X-ray machines I worked with. Sam and I struck up a friendship, and he shared about his faith in God. "You know, it's never too late to start a relationship with God," he told me. "It doesn't matter what your past looks like; he is always waiting with open arms."

I sighed. "Sam, it all sounds fine and dandy, but let's face it. My life is hard. I'm a single mother, struggling to make ends meet. You have a perfect life, and I can never be like you. Sorry, but I just don't see God being too interested in my life."

"Well, don't give up on him, because he won't give up on you," Sam pressed.

A co-worker approached me about my friendship with Sam. "You two are always arguing," she said with a laugh. "What's going on?"

I shook my head. "Oh, no, Sam's a good guy. I don't mind discussing this religious stuff, but he knows my views are very different from his."

"Oh, I see," she mumbled as she walked away.

One day, a guy named Mark from the purchasing department at work gave me a book. It discussed the Amway company and the multi-level marketing opportunity. I had always been open to being an entrepreneur and had even thought it might be fun to open up my own Hallmark retail store. I agreed to go out with Mark and his friends to see what this Amway thing was all about.

At dinner, I was surprised when Mark and his friends bowed their heads to pray. But I didn't object, and as we ate, I became intrigued with their conversation. They discussed God in a way I'd never heard people talk; it was as if Jesus was living in modern times, and he was their friend.

"I just love what God is doing in my life. He's teaching me new things every day," one guy said. "Whenever I get really discouraged, I know I can ask him to help me."

His words resonated with me. *Now this God they talk about just might be one I could buy into,* I decided.

I signed up for the Amway company and enjoyed all the connections and new friendships I made through it. One day, as I was out shopping at yard sales, I heard a song on the radio. "I will be your shelter, I'll give you my shoulder. Just reach out for my love, call my name, and my heart will be near. I will be there, there's nothing to fear …" came a deep, soothing voice through the speakers. After it was over, the DJ announced it was by Michael W. Smith.

I stopped by the record store later that afternoon and

asked the clerk where I could find the song. "Oh, that would be over in the Christian section," she said, motioning toward the wall.

That was a Christian song? I was amused as I picked up the record and purchased it. I went home, popped it in the stereo and listened as the music filled the room. The words were meaningful and yet not cheesy, and they stuck with me as I fell asleep. Slowly, my interest for all this God stuff was growing, but I didn't quite know what to do with it yet.

My friends in California had showed me a magazine called *Alaskan Men's Magazine*. Because women were so scarce in Alaska, the magazine was used as a matchmaking source. We had fun flipping through the pages and reading the various guy's biographies. Many of them seemed cute and interesting, but a particular one stood out to me. It was a guy in a wheelchair; his name was Bill. He had kind eyes and a nice smile, and I liked what he wrote about himself. I didn't give it much thought, though. I was a single working mother; the last thing I needed was to try dating.

One day, at a monthly Amway meeting, I saw a guy in a wheelchair who looked a lot like the guy in that magazine. The more I studied him, the more convinced I became that it was the same guy. *I'd really like to get to know him someday,* I decided. *He seems intriguing.*

As I got ready for bed one night, I suddenly thought to open up the Bible my grandmother had given me all those years ago. It was still brand-new, and the pages were crisp as I turned them. I wasn't quite sure what to look for as I read, but something inside me had been stirring, and I had a sudden urge to know more about this Jesus Sam told me about.

The next day at work, I told Sam I wanted to go with him to church. A smile spread across his face, and he told me he'd just been waiting for the day I'd ask.

To my surprise, everyone was especially friendly when I stepped through the church doors that Sunday morning. I leaned forward, hanging on the edge of my front row seat as the pastor shared from the pulpit. This was so different than the church services I'd visited as a child. The pastor talked about God just as my Amway friends did — as though he was a friend.

A few weeks later, I attended a nondenominational church service during a three-day Amway event. The pastor shared a simple message that resonated with me in my heart. "Every one of us has messed up and done wrong things. But the God of the Bible is a God of hope, a God of restoration. He knew we would all mess up in our lives, so he sent his son, Jesus, to earth to pay the price for our wrongdoings by dying on the cross. Being a Christian does not mean simply following a bunch of rules; it means enjoying a relationship with God. Through him, we can find lasting hope, peace and joy, and we can spend eternity with him in heaven."

That makes so much sense, I suddenly realized. When the pastor gave an invitation to come forward and invite Jesus into our lives, I shot out of my seat and raced to the front. I prayed in my heart that morning, asking God to direct my life and forgive me for the things I'd done wrong in my life. I now knew without a doubt that I needed God; I could not make it through life without him. He was the reason Sam and all my Amway friends were filled with so much joy. Now I could experience that joy for myself!

I shared my new faith with my kids, now 16 and 18 years old. "I know I spent years bashing the church and the people in it, but I now see what I've been missing all along," I told them excitedly. "I only hope you can find the peace I've discovered in my heart. God is the real deal."

My daughter, always dramatic, slapped her hand across her forehead. "So everything you told us was a lie, Mom?"

My son nodded slowly. "We're always talking about faith and God in Boy Scouts, but I always listened to you, Mom, and believed it was just a bunch of baloney. You're telling me it's all true?"

"Yes!" I exclaimed. It was as though someone had finally turned the light on in a dark room. The plain, wonderful truth had been in front of me the whole time. "Just read the Bible for yourself," I encouraged him. "You'll see that God is real. And hopefully you'll see him in my life as he works in my heart."

I joined a Bible study at church and enjoyed learning more about God. Everything was now so clear. God was not against me — he was *for* me! He wanted me to enjoy his peace and love, but he knew I could not live life on my own. That's why he so badly wanted me to enter into a relationship with him. All those years I had spent crying over my husband, beating my head against the wall because I was so distraught, I could have simply turned to God and asked him for help. He had been there all along. And he was here now, ready to show me the meaning of true love. My husband had let me down, but God would not do the same. God's love for us never changed.

One day, I drove out to the water to spend some time alone. I loved the sound of ocean waves, and though the rugged, chilly sea in Alaska was much different than the warm, sunny California one, it still brought me great comfort. As I sat there praying, I felt God say to me, *All those years ago, when you were crying in the bathroom, that was me talking to you.*

"It was, God?" I said aloud, stunned. I remembered the moment so clearly; I had been sure I'd never make it through the night with my abusive husband. But God had been there protecting me in that moment, and it was his voice I had heard. Even when I had not wanted anything to do with him, he had pursued me. And just as Sam had said, when I had given up on God, he had not given up on me. What a comfort!

One day, as I dropped my daughter off at her job at Kentucky Fried Chicken, I noticed a guy in a wheelchair waiting outside the grocery store next door. His daughter came out a few minutes later, and I racked my brain, trying to think of something to say to him. But nothing came to mind, and they got in their car and left.

I decided to buy Bill a card to congratulate him on his

recent accomplishments in Amway, wrote out a few sentences and popped it in the mailbox without signing my name. *Well, that's that,* I told myself. *I'm just going to go on with my life.*

When I was 43 years old, my son's friend Trevor told me excitedly, "I met this guy, and you've totally gotta go talk to him. He's got some really great business ideas. His name is Bill Johnson."

I recognized the name immediately, so of course, I agreed to meet with him. It was the same Bill Johnson I'd seen at the Amway meetings, in the magazine and at the grocery store. I felt a bit silly, as I knew so much about him and he knew nothing about me. But I was glad to finally be able to talk to him without any awkwardness. We hit it off, and I listened intently as he shared his business ideas. They were indeed good, and I agreed to a partnership with him and Trevor. In the meantime, I kept up my job at the hospital.

Bill was even warmer in person than I'd expected. I loved the way he laughed and loved his optimism for life. I learned that he had become disabled in a car accident in his 20s. His wife had left him years ago, and he had done his best to raise his daughter on his own. Bill had a strong faith in God and shared that it had sustained him during those difficult times.

The more I got to know Bill, the more I liked him. But something gnawed at me inside. If there was any chance of reconciliation with my husband, I felt like I needed to give it a chance. I returned to Southern California and tried to visit him, but he would not tell me where he was or let me see him. Frustrated, I returned to Alaska. *Well, God, I tried,* I thought resignedly.

Shortly after I returned, I got a devastating phone call. My husband had committed suicide. He had never found the hope in God I had, and wracked with guilt over his life, he had chosen to tragically end it without telling anyone.

How could he do such a thing, God? I prayed through my tears. I vacillated between anger and pity over the next few weeks as I grieved. He had left behind two children who would never know their father again. Life suddenly seemed terribly unfair.

I continued to pray and cry out to God, asking him to help me reconcile the pain in my heart. As terrible as my husband had been to me at times, he had still been my husband, and a tiny part of me had always hoped we might get back together. But now it was too late.

At work, I cried all the time, unable to get a hold of myself. The pettiness among my co-workers bothered me, and one day, unable to cope with it all, I walked out of my shift. I found a Christian counselor and began attending sessions. As I poured out my heart and cried, the counselor offered up great insight.

"Teri, you have spent much of your life running from your pain and your problems instead of facing things head-on. But it's now time to do just that. In the past, you tried to do it all on your own. But the wonderful thing is, now you have God," he reminded me.

"You're right," I said through my tears. "You're absolutely right."

Bill and Trevor remained by my side as I wrestled with my loss. I was grateful for such great friends who shared my hope in God. My son quietly handled his grief, while my daughter lashed out in her pain. I tried to console them the best I could, reminding them that there were some things in life we would never understand. I knew I was not promised an easy life, but I also knew that God would never leave me in my darkest hour. He was my strength and my hope.

That August, Bill asked me to go to his sister's for his birthday, and I agreed. After dinner, I decided to tell him about the card I'd sent. "I know this might sound silly, but it was me who sent you that anonymous card a while back," I told him shyly.

Bill laughed. "I knew it was you all along, Teri. You write just like you talk."

I stared at him. "You knew?" I asked incredulously.

He winked at me. "Yep. You stalker," he teased.

Bill and his daughter went to Anchorage and bought me an engagement ring, and we married a short time after. I had always been intrigued by people in wheelchairs and found their inner source of strength very appealing. In my heart, I knew Bill was the perfect man for me — kind-hearted, generous and hardworking. And best of all, he loved God more than he loved me.

I moved into Bill's house on a rural piece of property in Knik, 12 miles outside of Wasilla. I began attending

Bill's small church, Sunny Knik Chapel, and quickly fell in love with the people, the pastor and the environment. Bill had been attending the church since the beginning, when they met in a basement, and he had enjoyed watching it grow over the years. It seemed like the perfect place for me, too, as we embarked on our new life together. Everyone welcomed us as a couple, and I was excited to call it home.

Bill and I became not just life partners but business partners in new ventures as well. We took my background in the medical field and radiology and, with the help of some friends, opened a large radiology center in the Wasilla area. The center eventually grew to four centers, and I thanked God for opening doors for us to succeed. I had always enjoyed being generous, and I looked forward to giving back to the community.

One day, I began experiencing heart palpitations, and as the weeks went by, they grew worse. Scott, a technologist in one of our centers, performed an echocardiogram on my heart. I was nonchalant as he hooked me up to the machine, but moments later, his eyes grew wide.

"What is it?" I asked nervously.

"You need a doctor. A different doctor, I mean," he said. "This does not look right."

A full echocardiogram revealed severe calcification over my heart. "It looks like this has been building up for years," the doctor said slowly. "You have a genetic defect in your aortic valve; it only has two flaps. This is what's causing the buildup. You need surgery as soon as possible."

"Surgery? Are you sure?" What I'd thought was just a minor thing had suddenly turned into a matter of life or death! I went home and told Bill, and he agreed that I should seek out a surgeon right away.

But after doing our research, we learned that the procedure I'd need, called a Ross procedure, was very rare; no doctor in Alaska could perform it. I looked in other states and found a doctor in Austin, Texas, who agreed to do the surgery. The day we scheduled the surgery, Bill busted his femur climbing on his ATV. Horrified by the timing of it all, I told my husband, "I am not going to go through with this surgery if you can't be with me."

Thanks to God and Bill's orthopedic doctor, two weeks before Christmas in 2003, Bill and I made the trip south for my surgery. We prayed all the way down, asking God to please protect and heal me. The moment my anxiety grew, I reminded myself of all God had already gotten me through in my life. He would not leave me now.

The day before my surgery, a young man in a shop we visited stopped his work and prayed with us. "God, please be with this woman and comfort her during this time," he prayed. "May she know you are with her always."

The hospital staff was especially accommodating and brought in a full-sized bed for Bill to lie in while we both recovered. "What a pair we are, huh?" I laughed along with Bill as the doctors prepped me for surgery. "Wish me luck, okay?"

I thanked God for his intervention in this scary time. After I came out of the operation, the doctors reported it was successful, and we all breathed a sigh of relief.

"It's a good thing you came when you did, though," one doctor told me. "You would have most likely had a heart attack if you hadn't had this fixed."

Once again, I realized how God had worked everything together for good. Had I not fooled around with that ultrasound machine that afternoon, I might never have known how serious my condition was. God was truly watching over me.

We returned to Alaska and resumed our focus on the radiology centers. But as time went by, we encountered leadership problems with our partners, and the stress finally got to me. I decided we needed to step back from the business. It was a difficult decision, as I loved what I did, and I hadn't the faintest idea what the future held. But I clung to the Bible verse Jeremiah 29:11 that read, "For I know the plans I have for you, declares the Lord. Plans to prosper you and not to harm you, plans to give you a hope and a future." I would trust that God would provide for us and show us where to go next.

We went the next two years without an income, yet we were never without food or basic provisions. I worried Bill might lose his house, and that troubled me greatly. After getting injured years earlier, generous friends from all over the Wasilla area had raised enough funds to build him this house. I didn't want to be the cause of us losing it now. But instead of continuing to fret, I put my trust in

God. From emotional hardship to health problems and everything in between, God had been with me, even when I did not yet know him. He would not leave us hanging.

᷾᷾᷾

"You know, some days I feel like we live in a national park," I told Bill as we sat on our porch, looking out at the snowcapped mountains ahead. "I really do feel pretty lucky that I ended up here. And with you, of course."

"Ditto," Bill said, smiling up at me. "It hasn't all been easy, but I wouldn't trade our life for the world."

After I stepped down from our medical centers, Bill and I tried our hand at real estate investing. Though we lost money on an out-of-state deal, we eventually secured a few local properties, including one with three small rental cabins on site. We sold our medical business in 2011 and looked forward to using the profit to help others. God had sustained us during financial hardship, and I was grateful for the opportunity to trust fully in his provision.

We both love our simple life just outside Wasilla, complete with friends, our church and our four grandchildren. I'd never imagined my journey would take me from sunny Southern California to the rural wilderness of Alaska. There had been much heartache along the way, but there had also been much joy.

A chill in the air surfaced as Bill and I headed back inside. I glanced back once more and thought about the big, beautiful picture. Just down the road sat a Girl Scout camp. It had been my dream to live by one as a little girl, but I'd never imagined that all these years later, I'd find it here in Alaska. God had known the outcome of my story all along, and though I had not been searching for him, he had certainly been searching for me. Despite my once skeptical heart, God had not given up on me. He pursued me relentlessly, in all my moves and through all my worries, placing people all around me to show me his love. And in the end, that love won me over. In the end, love won.

A PRESENCE IN THE DARKNESS
The Story of Wanda Craig
Written by Karen Koczwara

"We can't stop the bleeding. We need another transfusion, quick."

"We're up to 16 pints now. What's going on?"

"Not sure, but it's not looking good."

The doctors' voices swirled above my head, a cacophony of frightening, confusing words. I lay there, too weak to speak up, feeling a bit like a science project under a microscope. Why could they not figure out how to stop the bleeding?

Machines buzzed, whirred and beeped around me in the sterile Intensive Care Unit, and somewhere down the hall, a doctor barked orders over the loudspeaker. I tried to take a deep breath to remind myself it would all be okay. This wasn't the first trial I had faced. I had known tragedy in my life; I had known great loss. But was this the end for me, or was there something else in store?

❧❧❧

I was born in 1935, making my debut in the middle of the Great Depression. Families across the country struggled to survive, many of them losing their homes, jobs and security as the world crashed down around them. But in the little town of Yakima, Washington, my mother, just 18 years old, faced a heartbreaking decision of her own.

Shortly before giving birth to me, my mother left my father, and she realized she could not care for me by herself in Eastern Washington. She sent me to live with her parents on their farm seven miles out of town, while she stayed in town and worked at the hospital full-time. She slept upstairs at the hospital when her long shift was over. Children were not allowed there, and every two weeks, she came to visit me on the farm.

I loved life at my grandparents' place. My mother's brother and older sisters still lived at home, and they provided endless entertainment. The farm encompassed 10 acres of fruit trees, crops and animals. I loved nothing more than spending my days outside, kicking up rocks, playing in the dirt and jumping off old tree stumps. The small house we all shared had no electricity, and an ice box served as our refrigerator down in the cellar. Though life was simple, I was content.

I loved cats more than any other animal. One day, one of our cats scampered far off into the orchards and refused to come back into the house. I told my grandmother he had escaped and grew worried he would not return before dark.

"I have an idea," she said with a smile. She slipped into the kitchen and returned a moment later with a warm homemade biscuit in her hand. My grandmother was famous for her soft, buttery biscuits, and when she had a batch of them in the oven, my nostrils tingled with delight.

"Try luring the cat back in the door with this," she suggested. "I'll bet he won't be able to resist."

I did as she instructed, leaving a trail of biscuit crumbs for the cat. Sure enough, he gobbled them up and bounded back into the house. I laughed, pleased to see that even the farm animals enjoyed my grandmother's cooking.

On Sundays, my grandparents took us to church. We all piled into my grandfather's Model T car; it had no windows but instead thick curtains to shield us from harsh weather.

One Sunday, as we rumbled down the road, a heavy storm blew in, and the rain pelted our faces and drenched our best dresses. By the time we arrived at church, my back was completely soaked, and I shivered as we filed into the building.

A potbellied stove sat in the middle of the old church building. My aunts and I marched over, lifted our dresses and stood against it until we were completely dry from its warmth. We then filed to the front of the church and took our places on the pew next to my grandparents. My grandmother always liked to sit up front, for she didn't want to miss a word the preacher said.

One Sunday morning, when I was 5, I sat quietly on the pew, trying my best to sit still. As the preacher read from his Bible, I glanced up and saw the strangest sight. A beautiful angel stood directly behind him, towering over him as he continued to preach. I had heard stories about angels and liked to sing about them at Christmastime, but

I had never actually seen one myself, until then. Tears filled my eyes as I stared straight ahead, mesmerized and speechless. An incredible peace came over my little heart, and I wondered if I was the only one who could see him.

My grandmother saw me crying and leaned over. "What are you crying for, child?" she asked.

I couldn't bring myself to answer her. *I'm too little,* I thought. *She'll never believe me.*

My mother married, but she still came to visit as often as she could. She became more of a sister to me, for in my heart, it was my grandmother I was closest to. One day, as I hung clothes on the line with my grandmother, we began to discuss church and God.

"You're 12, which means you're old enough to take communion now," she told me.

"Am I saved?" I blurted out. I had heard many church people discuss "getting saved." So far as I understood it, getting saved meant inviting God's son, Jesus, into your life so that you could have a relationship with him and go to heaven someday. I knew that I believed in God and that I had seen an angel, but I wasn't sure if I'd truly invited him into my life.

"If you don't know if you are saved, then you're not," my grandmother replied. "But it's not something to be scared of. Jesus wants all of us to have a relationship with him. He knows that none of us is perfect; we are going to mess up lots of times. But he loves us so very much and wants us to spend eternity with him in heaven after we die someday. That's why he came to earth to die on the cross for the wrong things we've done. You'll know when you're ready to talk to God and invite him into your life."

It all still sounded a bit confusing to me. A few weeks later, we took a trip to Seattle to visit a sick friend. During our stay, my aunt took me and my grandparents to the local church. As the service began, the preacher prayed for those who were ailing, and out of nowhere, tears streamed down my face.

My grandmother's friend came down the aisle and approached us. "Do you think she'd like to go up front and talk to God with me?" she asked my grandmother, nodding toward me.

Suddenly, I knew just what I wanted to do. I followed the woman to the front, knelt and said a simple but heartfelt prayer, inviting Jesus to come into my life. "I know I still have lots to learn, but I know that you are real, and I want to live for you. Thank you for dying on the cross to save me from all the wrong things I've done," I prayed softly. "Help me to obey you and share your love with others."

That night, as we drove home, I felt a newfound peace in my heart. My body felt lighter, the grass seemed greener and even the stars shined brighter. I felt like I'd just met my new best friend, and I could hardly wait to spend the rest of my life with him.

Excited about my new relationship with God, I spent hours a day reading my Bible and praying. I took my Bible to school and flipped through it during lunchtime, and the minute I got home, I flopped on my bed and opened the pages. As I read the stories, they all came alive, and it thrilled me to think that the God in the pages of this book was the same God who wanted to get to know me, a simple 12-year-old farm girl with still so much to learn.

One night, as I prayed at church, I felt God speak to me in my heart. *Someday, you will go to Alaska,* he told me.

Alaska! I had never been to Alaska before; I had barely left our little town in 12 years. I had heard it was beautiful, though, with tall snowy mountains, blue skies and wildlife unlike anything I'd seen on the farm. Would I really end up there someday? And if so, what would be waiting for me when I arrived?

Because we lived 12 miles from the local school, I had to take the bus into town every day. One particular girl picked on me relentlessly, tossing my books into puddles and calling me cruel names. When I mentioned her to my grandfather, he told me that I must never fight back or try to defend myself; I must simply ignore her. But it was difficult to turn the other way when she refused to leave me alone, and my anxiety grew each time I mounted the steps to the school bus.

One afternoon, as the bus rumbled down the road, the mean girl slid into the seat next to me and pushed my books out of my hand. "Nice dress," she sneered, glancing down at my outfit with disdain. "You're nothin' but a poor farm girl, aren't you?"

My eyes welled with tears, but I fought them back. I remembered my grandfather's words; I must not retaliate.

Instead, I turned away, but she kicked me swiftly in the leg, then grabbed my head with both hands and slammed it against the bus window as hard as she could. I winced in pain and couldn't help but scream out.

"Ooh, did that hurt, you little baby?" she hissed in my ear, laughing.

"Shut up, okay? Just leave me alone!" I had reached my boiling point. I could not take her bullying any longer.

"Girls! Both of you! Up here now!" the bus driver shouted. "Come sit down on the steps by the door for the rest of the ride. Enough horseplay!"

Humiliated, I hung my head as I trudged to the front of the bus and plopped onto the hard, cold steps. The mean girl sat down beside me, and I avoided her eyes as we bounced up and down. When she got off, I breathed a sigh of relief, but I kept my head hung, too embarrassed to face the rest of my peers on the bus. When would the torture ever end?

I was relieved when the mean girl was sent off to another school; she would never bother me again. Though rattled by her incessant taunting, I focused on my schoolwork and my new friends. I secured a spot in the school play in eighth grade and enjoyed my few moments in the spotlight. I only wished I lived closer to town so I could get involved with extracurricular activities. Though living on a farm was an adventure, it also made my teenage social life a bit challenging.

When I was 15 years old, a couple of boys my age stopped by my grandparents' house. They had just killed a large deer while out hunting and were anxious to show it off.

"That's quite a nice catch you got there," my grandfather observed, checking out the bloody buck.

I hovered at the doorway, more intrigued by the cute boys than the deer. Little did I know one of those boys would play an important part in my life story someday.

In high school, I got a job at the local hospital prepping trays of food for 140 patients. To bring in extra money, I tramped through the muddy fields, picking raspberries and strawberries and hoeing rows during harvest season. I wasn't sure what I wanted to do with my life, but I was certain that I wanted to be able to provide for myself. I had seen my mother struggle over the years, and I didn't want to live like that.

When I was 17, my mother came back to my grandparents' to live with us. She had left her husband and was trying to start her life over again. My mother had become like a big sister to me, so I enjoyed her company the best I could but did not look to her for advice or provision. After a year, she moved on with her life again, and I moved on with mine.

One Sunday morning, a man came to church and shared about a Bible college in nearby Everett, Washington. "It's only a five-month program, but it's a great way to really get to know your Bible more and grow closer to God," he explained. "If you're interested, I'd be happy to tell you more after the service."

My ears perked up. Since inviting Jesus into my life, I

had enjoyed a close relationship with him, reading my Bible each day and talking to him just as I'd talk to a dear friend. Whenever I grew anxious or upset, he was the first one I turned to for help. I felt his peace in my heart, and though I could not physically see him, I sensed his presence throughout every day. The idea of going to school to learn even more about God excited me greatly.

I discussed it with my friend, and she agreed to go with me; we'd live together. I ran the idea past my grandparents, and they agreed it would be good for me to broaden my world. And so I packed my bags, ready to embark on a new adventure at the age of 19.

I kept a busy schedule at Bible college, studying diligently in the evenings and attending classes during the day. On the weekends, I kept up my job at the hospital. My mother sometimes came to visit. She picked up my dirty clothes, washed them and brought them back to me. I was grateful for her support. I knew that despite not being able to raise me on her own, she had always done the best she could.

One day while working at the hospital, I met a cute guy. We struck up a conversation and developed a friendship. Soon, we began dating, and I fell hard for him. We married when I was just 20 years old, and not long after the wedding, I discovered I was pregnant. With Bible college now completed, it was time to enjoy the next chapter of my life.

Just a month after we married, my grandmother got a blood clot in her leg and suddenly passed away. Two weeks later, my grandfather passed away unexpectedly, too. Their deaths left me reeling; they had been like parents to me since I was born, and now they were both gone in an instant. How would I fill the gaping hole in my heart?

Despite my grief, life marched on. My new husband was a shrimp boat fisherman. His work required him to spend time on the coast of Florida, so I saw very little of him during our early years. When I gave birth to my first child, I was happy for him to be there with me. We resumed life as a family for a short while before he left again. I gave birth to three more children, one every September for the next three years. Soon, our home was filled with laughter and chaos, as little ones crawled at my feet and climbed into my lap. But despite the constant noise, a loneliness crept into my heart. I didn't know how much longer I could go on living as a single mother most of the year.

One evening, I crossed paths with an old acquaintance. I vaguely recognized him, but as we began chatting, I realized where I'd seen him before. "You came to my grandmother's years ago with that deer you'd killed!" I exclaimed.

"That's right. Good to see you again, Wanda!" Don had stayed in the Washington area over the years. Tall and broad-shouldered, he was a man's man who liked to hunt and fish. I found him handsome and intriguing, but I didn't think anything of our visit; I was a married woman.

I tried moving down to Florida for a year to be with

my husband, but our marriage did not improve. The distance between us was not just geographical; it was emotional, too. After seven years of trying to make things work, we finally parted ways. I was now officially left to raise four young children on my own, and once again, I turned to God for help. He was the only one who could sustain me through this difficult time.

When I was 28 years old, I went to visit my father. I was nervous and excited all at once. Since he had never been in my life, God had become my heavenly father. But I had thought about him many times over the years and wondered what he was like. Did we share the same mannerisms? The same likes and dislikes? Did I have his eyes or his hair color or his skin type? He had remained a mystery to me my whole life, and I was anxious to see if we had anything in common.

To my pleasant surprise, my father was more like me than I expected. We were both short, with blue eyes and dark hair. As we chatted over dinner, I watched him carefully as he spoke. He raised his brows, waved his hands and smiled just like me. *We both have the same quirky expressions*, I thought to myself with a smile. A mixture of sadness and elation overcame me as I wished I could have gotten to know this man more when I was a child.

"I haven't gotten to travel as much as I would have liked to in my life, but I do really enjoy getting postcards and letters from people all over the world," he told me.

"Me, too!" I cried. "I have a whole stack of postcards

I've saved over the years. I love going to the mailbox and finding out where the latest one has come from. I write missionaries sometimes, too, and enjoy hearing about all their adventures."

"Boy, we really are alike, aren't we? No doubt you're my daughter," my father said with a soft smile. "You know, I never married after your mother and I separated, and I wished many times for a family. But I am glad we're sitting here now, face to face. It's never too late for first encounters, is it?"

It's never too late. His words stuck with me as we said our goodbyes. I was newly divorced with four young children and little means to survive. I had felt God tell me I'd one day go to Alaska, but I was still in Washington. Though my situation felt disheartening, I trusted that God's timing was better than mine. I had read in the Bible that he had a plan for each of our lives and that while we often didn't understand his ways, he always knew what was best in the end.

Don and I reconnected, and our new friendship quickly blossomed into more. He was divorced as well and had a daughter, so he knew the struggles that came with single parenthood. After just one month, we decided to marry. He took excellent care of me and the children, and I was grateful God had brought him back into my life. I knew Don did not have a relationship with God, but I prayed for him every day and hoped that one day he would want what I had.

Every Sunday, Don drove me and the kids to church

and dropped us off. "I will never beg you to invite God into your life," I told him. "I gave you up to him, and I am just going to continue to pray for you." I respected Don as a husband, father and leader of our home, and I was confident that if he saw my genuine love for him and for God, he would discover the greatest gift I'd ever received.

Don and I had four more children over the years. He worked in the heavy construction industry, building roads and bridges. Our home was now bustling with babies, teenagers and everything in between. When I was 35, I developed diabetes, which made every day a bit more challenging. But I pressed on, thanking God for strength when I was weary. And each Sunday, I took the kids to church by myself and continued to pray for my husband. I would tell him often, "If you don't go to church, the church will one day come to you!"

One evening as we headed in for dinner, we noticed a bear staring down our cow out back. "That cow is never going to come in on its own," I told the kids. "We're gonna have to go out and get it."

We raced back outside and quickly untied the cow. Though we were moving fast, that cow beat us back to the house! When we got to the front door, she stuck her hind legs up, and we soon realized she wanted in the house. She was trying to climb the front steps! We thought quickly and corralled her into the dog pen to keep her safe. "That was a close one," I said, laughing as we shut the door. "Never a dull moment out here!"

I found a church to attend and continued taking the

kids on my own. One day, one of the couples from our church asked if they could hold services in our home.

"Of course!" I agreed. I went home and told Don the news.

"If you don't go to church, the church will come to you!" he said with a smile.

For the next two years, we met with two other couples weekly in our home. Don sat quietly in the corner, observing from a distance as we prayed, read the Bible and shared what God had been doing in our lives. And eventually, he decided he wanted to invite this Jesus I'd shared with him into his life. I cried tears of joy, for it had been more than 20 years since I'd first started praying for him. That night, I thanked God for answering those prayers, grateful I had never given up on him.

I enjoyed watching the man I already loved so much grow in his new relationship with God. Though he had always been a peaceful man, he now exuded true joy, and it spilled over into our marriage. I was thrilled that we were finally able to share the one thing I'd held most important in my life since I was 12 years old.

At night, we all gathered around an old piano, and I played while the family sang. And as the sun set, the children raced around outside, playing Indian wars and other creative games.

As much as I loved our simple life in the wild, I knew in my heart that I was still made for more. I had been so sure in my heart that God was leading me up to Alaska to serve him in some way.

A PRESENCE IN THE DARKNESS

As my children grew up, they moved away to start families and lives of their own. One of my sons moved to Alaska, where he began homesteading on a plot of land. Homesteading, in which residents attempted to sustain themselves off their land, had become increasingly popular in rural places of Alaska over the previous few years. One day he called to ask me if we'd like to move up to live with him.

I had continued to pray about Alaska over the years and had never given up on the idea. But living in such a remote area wasn't exactly what I had in mind. "I don't know," I told him with uncertainty.

"If I had a house for you, would you move?" my son pressed.

"Well, I suppose that would change things."

"You think about it, Mom. If you decide to try it, I'll come down and help you move."

I prayed about it and felt God was giving us the green light; it was finally my time! "Don, we're moving to Alaska," I told my husband. "Let's start packing!"

Two weeks after my son called, we piled all our belongings into our white van and made the trek north. We drove down a muddy, narrow dirt road and arrived at a tiny cabin in a remote area called Rufus Creek. The building had no running water, very little lighting and a simple wood stove for cooking. I took one look around and thought with dismay, *What have we gotten ourselves into?* Eventually, my son and his wife moved on to another place, and we added on to the tiny cabin to create more space. Life in the rugged wilderness soon grew on me. I enjoyed the newfound simplicity, the gorgeous Alaskan sky and the vast green terrain that surrounded us from all angles.

ॐॐॐ

As we entered our later years, things shifted dramatically. We were now grandparents, and our home, once bustling with constant noise and laughter, was often quiet in the evenings. But Don and I enjoyed each other's company and the slower-paced life we now lived. We planted several new crops and watched excitedly as they sprouted up. It had taken me many years to get up here, but Alaska now truly felt like home.

"I think we're going to have a great crop this year," I told Don one night as we glanced out the window at our blooming fields. Up above, the stunning northern lights shone bright, the rugged mountains a perfect backdrop to the Alaskan sky. Everything seemed to be in its rightful place.

And then one day in 1994, my husband suddenly passed away of a heart attack. My faithful companion was gone, and a little piece of my own heart broke off and died along with him. I resumed life, grateful for my church friends who kept me company during the long, lonely days. And I thanked God that, despite it all, he was the one constant thing in my life, the only one who would never leave or fail me.

I tried to keep up our land and our crops, but my son and I had our hands full. The soil was particularly acidic, and the bugs were more prevalent than ever. One afternoon, as I worked in the fields, I suddenly felt weak. I tried to walk across the road to a neighbor's house, but every step was a struggle. When I arrived, I was completely out of breath. And that was just the beginning.

After undergoing several tests at the hospital, the doctors announced that the very thing that had killed Don had nearly killed me. I would need a quadruple bypass heart surgery!

"Heart surgery?" I gasped. "I'm only 61 years old!"

"And lucky to be alive," the doctor reminded me. "We'll schedule you as soon as possible."

I survived the surgery, but as the doctors predicted, my recovery was slow. My daughter Freida lived in Wasilla 250 miles away and suggested I come live with her.

"You can't stay out there on that land alone, Mom," she told me. "We'll take care of you."

I agreed to move in with her. It was difficult to leave the place we'd called home for so many years, as we'd made many memories there. But my daughter was right; I could not live alone. What if something happened to me again?

Though it was an adjustment, I soon came to enjoy the little suburban town of Wasilla. I began attending Sunny Knik Chapel and loved the friendly folks at the church. But just as I gained back my strength, I received another round of devastating news. In 2004, I found out my daughter, now living in Colorado, was dying of liver and bone cancer. In 2008, my son, who had moved to Northern Oregon to become a preacher, found out he had a brain tumor. Within four years of each other, they were both gone. My world was completely rocked as I grieved their losses. I had sustained so much already — big moves, the death of my husband and major heart surgery. But nothing could have prepared me for this.

"God, I need your strength more than ever," I prayed through my tears. "Only you can get me through this terrible time of grief."

As I prayed, I felt his presence, strong and fierce, as though he was wrapping me in his arms with the warmth of his love. Though my life once again felt uncertain and bleak, I knew that God, my heavenly father, would never leave my side. He had promised me through his words in the Bible that nothing could separate me from his love. It would be him and only him who would sustain me through these tragedies.

పోపోపో

"Hmm." The doctor's brow furrowed, and a look of concern spread over his face as he walked around the side of the hospital bed. "Did you fall recently, Wanda?"

I shook my head. "No. Why?"

"Well, your back is all purple. It looks as though you have some internal bleeding going on. I'm concerned about this and need to find out where it's coming from."

A PRESENCE IN THE DARKNESS

My heart jumped in my chest. It was late August 2011. I was now 75 years old and had lived alone for the past several years in a little two-bedroom apartment in Wasilla. I enjoyed my simple life, which included visits with my kids, church on Sundays and dinners out with the church ladies at local restaurants. I also led a Bible study every Wednesday morning in my home and loved sharing God's love with everyone I met. Despite my heartache, God had given me a renewed sense of hope over the years, and I was grateful to be serving him in Alaska, just as I'd prayed I would do as a young girl.

Just a few weeks before, I had grown suddenly weak and tired. Determined to find out why I had no stamina, I visited the doctor, who confirmed that I had high levels of Coumadin, a medicine prescribed to prevent heart attacks and blood clots, and very high potassium levels. It was during this doctor's visit that things suddenly took a turn for the worse.

The doctor admitted me to the local hospital for a few days to monitor my failing kidneys. I was used to living alone in my quiet apartment, but the noisy hospital, with its buzzing machines and loudspeaker announcements, seemed somehow lonelier than ever. I lay in bed, waiting and praying as the minutes slowly ticked by on the clock across the room.

"God, I don't know what's going on inside of me, but you do," I prayed. "Please give the doctors some answers soon."

I drifted off to sleep, and when I awoke, I saw a man

standing next to my bed, watching me closely. He had dark skin, dark eyes and weathered skin that looked as if it had seen plenty of sun. I rubbed my bleary eyes and realized just who it was — it was Jesus! Too stunned to say anything, I just lay there, mesmerized by his kind eyes. I had read plenty of stories about Jesus in the Bible and had seen pictures of him in storybooks as a child. I'd always assumed he had light skin, but I now realized that of course he would have darker skin; he was a Jewish Middle-Eastern man.

A mixture of comfort and excitement overcame me in my weakened state. When I blinked my eyes again, he was still standing there, looking down on me as a father would on his sleeping child. He said nothing, nor did I, but it did not matter; his presence was simply enough. Jesus, the one I had invited into my heart as a young girl, was standing at the foot of my bed, watching over me! He had not forsaken me in this lonely hospital room; instead, he was right by my side. What a wondrous thing!

I drifted back to sleep, and when I awoke, my daughter Freida was at the foot of my bed. "Guess what?" I whispered, a smile breaking over my face. "I saw Jesus! He was standing right where you are, watching over me with a smile!"

Freida's eyes filled with tears. "Oh, Mom, I believe you! That's wonderful!" she cried.

I knew without a doubt that no matter the outcome of my health journey, I did not need to fear. If I died, I would go to be with Jesus, and he would welcome me with loving arms when I got to heaven. And if I remained on earth for a few more years, he would still wrap me in those loving arms and comfort me every step of the way.

"This is definitely no bedsore," the doctor said when he came back to check on me. "We're going to have to give you a blood transfusion. Your back is even more purple, and we have to stop the bleeding before it worsens. Unfortunately, we have to take you off the Coumadin. Because of the micro valve they put in during your past heart surgery, the bleeding could go to your brain if you remain on the Coumadin. It seems your kidneys are failing, too, so we're going to put in a catheter right away."

Everything was happening so quickly. I did not understand all the doctor lingo, but I knew I had to simply trust that the doctors knew what they were doing and that God knew the ultimate outcome.

Despite the transfusion, I continued to bleed. Still baffled by my condition, the doctors decided to move me to another hospital. They hoisted me onto an ambulance, and as it sped down the road, the paramedics pressed a brick against my shoulder for added pressure to minimize the blood loss from the catheter. I continued to pray in my weakened state, asking God to give me a spirit of peace in this uncertain time.

The next few hours were a blur of confusion. Once I arrived at Providence, a nurse checked me in and took my vitals. "How old are you?" she asked me.

"I'm 75," I whispered.

She suddenly noticed that I had started bleeding

through the catheter. "I'm going to call for a doctor right away," she said swiftly, then walked off.

But the doctor did not arrive. I lay in the bed, waiting, the beeping and buzzing and whirring of the machines lulling me to sleep. When I awoke, the clock on the wall read 11 p.m. I had been there since 6 p.m., and still no one had come to my aid. Panic began to rise in my chest, but I was too weak to do anything. *God, help me. Please bring a doctor soon.*

At last, when it was nearly midnight, a doctor arrived to check on me. "What's going on?" he asked as he checked me out. "I'm going to take this catheter out with scissors, okay? Just hang tight."

I helped administer pressure after he removed the catheter. "They had to give me blood transfusions at the other hospital," I told him.

"Well, you've lost half that blood already," he said somberly. "You might need another transfusion if the bleeding doesn't stop."

I had learned through life's hardships and tragedies that when circumstances were out of my control, I only had one place to go. I simply had to turn to Jesus and trust in him. There was no other answer in times like these; only he could bring me peace.

As I lay there, weak, disoriented and exhausted, a piece of a Bible verse I'd once heard came to my mind. *I will sing of the mercies ...* I tried to think of the rest, but I could not finish the sentence. Instead, I drifted off to sleep.

After a flurry of testing, poking and more testing, the

doctors finally decided to put the catheter back in and slowly start the Coumadin again. They explained that I had been bleeding from my kidneys, and after administering a total of 16 pints of blood, they finally got the bleeding to subside. They administered oxygen to help me breathe steadily and started me on dialysis to get my kidneys functioning again.

Many friends from church came to visit me in the hospital and bring flowers. One day my pastor arrived to check in on me. "God gave me part of a verse, but I can't remember the rest," I whispered to him. I had a tiny fine-print Bible at my bedside but had lost my glasses. I shared the portion of the verse with my pastor, and he nodded his head.

"Psalm 89:1. It reads, 'I will sing of the mercies of the Lord forever, with my mouth I will make known thy faithfulness to all generations.'"

"That's it!" I said excitedly. "That's the verse!"

I completely lost my voice and was only able to talk to my kids in a hoarse whisper when they called to check on me. I remained in the hospital for the next month. The warm August summer days waned outside my hospital window, and the crisp September air ushered in the first hint of fall. At last, on September 23, the doctors released me to go home. They strictly ordered that I must not be left alone and must remain under care 24 hours a day.

My daughter, grandchildren and close friends took shifts caring for me. I continued on dialysis, and a nurse came in twice a week to check my vitals. Each day, I gained a bit more strength, and by October, I was finally able to leave my house and attend church.

I had missed being in church more than anything. Concerned friends rushed up to say hello and tell me they'd been praying for me. We exchanged hugs and a few tears, and I thanked God once again for bringing me to Wasilla so that I could find such a great group of people who loved me and loved him.

I was still too weak to stand or raise my hands as we sang, but as the worship songs echoed through the room, I felt God say to me, *In my time, all things work together for good.* I thanked him for these words and chose to believe that he would work all of my trials together for his good — in his perfect timing.

On October 20, I called a dear friend from Washington. As I gave her an update on my health, she said, "I believe God wants you to know something. I have a special message from him, and it is this: 'Daughter of Zion, rise up, rise up. It is not your time. You have a word to say.'"

"Wow," I whispered, a smile spreading across my face. "I guess God has bigger plans for me."

I continued dialysis, but as November neared, I felt God say to me, *By your birthday, you will be healed.* My birthday was in December; would I truly be healed after years of struggling with my health? I believed in my God, though, and I believed that he could work miracles, because I had seen him do it before. I would just have to wait on him and see.

A PRESENCE IN THE DARKNESS

On November 21, just before Thanksgiving, I had another round of dialysis. Halfway through, I had the sudden urge to go to the bathroom. "Nurse, I need to go to the bathroom!" I told her urgently.

The nurse glanced at the clock. "You can't. You have 19 minutes left of your treatment," she replied, shaking her head.

But I was certain God was healing me; I would not need dialysis much longer.

On December 23, the dialysis head nurse had good news for me. "Wanda, this is your last treatment," she said with a smile. "You won't need to come back anymore."

I praised God for healing me one step at a time. What a wonderful early Christmas present!

On February 28, 2012, the doctors removed my catheter for good and gave me a clean bill of health. I thanked God once again. He had promised me I would be healed before my birthday, and I was! He had sustained me through one of the scariest experiences of my life, but he had never once forgotten me. And when I was at my weakest and loneliest, he had sent Jesus to my side to bring comfort. I would never forget the image of the man with the weathered, dark skin and kind eyes smiling down on me. God had given me a second chance at life, and I knew my journey wasn't over. It was time to share my story with the world!

≈≈≈

"Wanda! So good to see you out and about! You look great!" my friends called as I entered the restaurant.

"Thank you. I feel great." I smiled as I took my seat at the table. The aroma of Asian stir fry wafted through the air, and my mouth watered. Since regaining my appetite over the last few months, I looked forward to going out to dinner with the ladies from church more than ever.

God had worked a miracle in me since my health scare the year before. I was now off most of my medications and had lost nearly 50 pounds. At 76 years old, I felt better than I had in decades. I maintained a healthy diet, took vitamins and supplements and stayed active leading Bible studies at home. Sunny Knik Chapel had become such a special place to me over the years, especially after losing my husband and two children. The wonderful members had become my family, and I looked forward to seeing them every Sunday morning when the pastor's wife picked me up for church. People often stood during the service to share what God had done in their lives, and I enjoyed their encouraging stories. They had all prayed for me during my darkest time, and I enjoyed praying for them, too.

As I looked around the table at my dear friends, I thanked God again for bringing me to Alaska. I had not known, at 12 years old, where my journey would take me, but God had known all along. He had not promised me an easy life when I invited him into my heart, but he had never once left my side. When circumstances seemed bleak and uncertain, I had felt his presence most, comforting me along the way.

I like to often tell people, "I am just between miracles." It seems a good way to sum up my life. God was always up to something. And I had a hunch my story was far from over.

REPLANTING HERITAGE
The Story of Duane Guisinger
Written by Richard Drebert

Despair split me open like buckshot, and I hoped that Alaska barrens might hide me from shame. Back home my wife and children lived on charity. I had squandered everything I held dear.

My jet boat screamed up the glistening Kanektok River, but in my mind, I lived in a dark basement room. I levered down the RPMs, and my two fishermen, clinging to $500 fishing rods, lurched drunkenly, laughing. They imbibed 90-proof *wilderness*, without a hint of alcohol, and watching them fumble with their tackle lightened my heart a tad. For $5,000 per head, our guide service offered cheechakos (greenhorns) a supervised experience camping in the wilds of the Last Frontier. But I teetered too near the jaws of desperation to enjoy Alaska. Wilderness grandeur scarcely staunched the bleeding in my heart anymore.

Nowhere in the world could fishermen revel in such a variety of indigenous, powerful fish caught in a single river — rainbows, grayling, Dolly Varden — and from June through August our clients shared five different species of salmon with Togiak grizzlies.

My father's stern face splashed across my memory as I positioned the boat for casting into a pool teeming with salmon ...

I was barely 18 when I worked my first horrific week at one of Oregon's busiest sawmills, Crown Zellerbach. My father had landed me a job on what lumbermen call the "green chain": stacking sappy, heavy dimensional timbers in segregated piles for grouchy foremen.

My soft hands were blistered, and my shoulders ached worse than any weight training I experienced in high school. At lunch break I stared longingly across the mill where men held clipboards or drove forklifts.

"How do I get one of those jobs, like them?" I asked my father, whose dependability and seniority over decades garnered him a position operating a massive circular saw.

"You have to earn it, Duane. Work your way to the other end of the mill …"

I watched my two fishermen cast into a riffle, and I wondered if I had the backbone anymore, to work to the "other end" of my desolation. I did seem to be making *some* headway.

At least I wasn't asking God to kill me anymore …

ಞಞಞ

I loved Dawn the day I met her at Bible camp. She was 12 years old, and I fell for her hook, line and sinker. I was 14, and in the two years that we sorta dated (she lived 170 miles away), I knew we were meant for each other. No other girl was as beautiful or kind or fun to be with. As often as I could, I rode a Greyhound to her town or she visited friends near me so we could see each other. But a long-distance romance is hard to keep alive.

One evening, I called Dawn to find out when to meet her at the Kelso bus station, and her sweet voice seemed … aloof. I cradled the receiver like a zombie.

"I'm sorry, Duane. You're so far away — and *he's* right here. Try to understand."

I didn't.

Apiary, Oregon, nestled in Douglas fir timber in the shadow of Mt. St. Helens, wasn't so idyllic after that. I was 16 years old, and I became obsessed with joining the Navy or living in some cabin with my horse, my rifle and pack. And Dawn wasn't my only problem. Dad and I were butting heads about school, chores and everything lately.

I needed an adventure, like Grandpa Archibald experienced. He had worked in Ketchikan, Alaska, as a machinist for the remote fish canneries. I never really knew him (I recalled his graveside funeral when I was 3), but I heard about him from Grandma Grace, who sat by me at our Pentecostal church every Sunday.

"Amazing Grace, how sweet the sound …" Oh, how I loved Grandma's lilting soprano voice, and she loved mine. At 16, if I hadn't had my singing gigs and Grandpa's old guitar, I might have gone stark-raving nuts!

With six whiney sisters and one little brother, I helped Mom bear the responsibility of childrearing, and my part meant bossing and tormenting them.

It took five years for Dad and Mom to build their dream home, and we excitedly moved from our teeny log house into a four-bedroom home that, to us, seemed like a mansion.

I had my own room then, a place to hole up and practice my country and church songs. I often exclaimed to myself, "Glory to Jesus!" like Sister Rose Fiddler always declared. (Sister Fiddler was an icon among local Pentecostals, famous for her wisdom and scrumptious apple pies.)

Working overtime at Crown Zellerbach was as natural for Dad as lacing up his big leather boots, and he added more hours every time Mom had a new baby. It's a miracle that he found days to school me in being a woodsman, and he was at my shoulder when I killed my first buck (a mile or more from our pickup). Dad sliced the legs to strap 'em together as a venison backpack, and he huffed all the way back to the truck with my buck on his back.

All he said was, "A hunter needs to *plan* where he shoots his game, son."

My father always seemed to carry a map of the future. He maintained control in every situation, and I assumed that God endorsed his lifestyle. From my father, the hard-driving Guisinger way of living soaked into me, like dried blood into a wool coat. And like Dad's father before him, I'd never stray from doing what I figured was the right thing.

As weary as my father must have felt after working so many hours, he never missed church. Mom and he tossed the eight of us into the big Ford station wagon, then herded us into God's sanctuary like a flock of ducklings. The wiggly Guisingers filled up a whole pew.

But sometimes Dad wasn't as perfect as everyone thought ...

When Mom won a contest at the downtown carpet store, she convinced him that it was only fair to have a family drawing, to see who got the carpet for his or her bedroom. He drew a name out of a hat, and glory be, I won!

No more cold feet in the morning! I could almost feel the carpet between my toes, until Dad settled us all down. He hated the thought of Mom and him losing out on new carpeting for *their* bedroom.

"Mmm. Whaddya think? Best two out of *three*?"

My sisters hopped around like gleeful bunnies, enjoying the shocked expression on my face. Our names got mixed around in the hat again, and Mom's hand dipped in. Guess who won — again?!

I loved my new carpet. I loved that I one-upped my dad even more.

When I was a kid, I never knew my father to make a mistake that he admitted, and I believed that it was because he held a position with God.

When I was 10, I picked up some Pentecostal Hellfire Insurance by telling God I was sorry for the bad things I did. But shame still troubled me. Every day I fell short of living up to the Bible rules, and I hoped to earn a better heaven-bound position as I grew to be a man. Sometimes Mom took me to community events and local clubs so I could perform, and I sang at services with preachers and chaplains at the county jail. The closest I got to feeling near Jesus was when I sang and played guitar.

It wasn't until I worked with Dad at Crown Zellerbach that I met the man that hard-case loggers respected and looked to for guidance. Dad's power seemed to come from something inside him, stronger than Hellfire Insurance.

"Say, Deacon. I got a kid down with pneumonia. Can you pray for him?" Dad always stopped right where he was to petition God on behalf of anyone who had a need. It was obvious my father possessed a mysterious kind of relationship with Jesus that I didn't have, and I determined to work even harder to get it.

My father hoped that I would carry on the Guisinger tradition, learning the sawmill from end to end. But I plotted my escape from the green chain to see the world — and my mother helped me find a way.

∽∽∽

"Fish on!" The little pear-shaped CEO had waited his whole life to yell those words in the Alaska bush.

"Keep your tip up, Mr. Rawlings. Reel in slow …" I knew he had a good-sized king salmon on the hook, and I mothered him with directions until netting the weary fish.

If Mr. Rawlings could have danced in our boat, he would have.

"Thank you! Thank you, Duane!"

"No, no. You did the hard work."

I had confidence that I could always guide my clients to big fish on the winding Kanektok River — but these days, that's where my faith ended.

I walk through the Valley of the Shadow of Death ...

And I had been on this path for months.

When I moved to Alaska, nearly 10 years before working the Kanektok River as a fishing guide, I felt certain I was doing what God wanted me to do. I was answering the call that God had for me. A pressing need to steer all my decisions by God's divine compass consumed me.

But now I nearly drowned in self-doubt.

I feel empty. Dead inside. Drained. Alone.

In a season of deep depression, I had flushed away years of ministry. I took to my bed in a basement apartment *done in*, wanting to die.

It was raining pretty hard, and my fishermen were soaked. "Shall we hit another hole or put our chef to work on lunch?" I knew their answers.

We sped back to our camp, where other clients milled around a crackling camp stove. The aroma of frying salmon steaks drifted in the wet breeze, and the atmosphere shouted *fulfillment. Absolute satisfaction.*

I remembered a time when I experienced fulfillment. Strangely enough, I discovered true happiness while serving in the U.S. Navy ...

Mom had driven me to the recruiter herself! I signed up for Navy Reserves and boarded a plane for boot camp, glad to leave my hometown of Rainier in the sawdust. I wanted to see the world from aboard a U.S. battleship.

Wanderlust had bitten me while Dad and I fished on the banks of the Columbia River. The blast of a freighter's horn signaled farewell to Oregon as it steamed to the open seas, and I imagined myself aboard, heading to Hawaii or other distant ports of call.

Months after Navy boot camp, my childhood dream partially came true. I found myself in Hawaii, tangled up in red tape as I waited for training in communications. I ended up aboard a ship called *Observation Island*, a testing craft for Polaris missiles.

But scraping paint off grimy decks wasn't what I signed up for — especially on a boat welded forever to a dock. My dreams of seeing foreign ports were dying in the depths of Pearl Harbor.

When a billet opened up for training as a dental technician/medic, I jumped at the chance.

"What experience have you had in the medical field, Guisinger?"

I rifled through ranch memories and recalled my prowess as a veterinarian's aide. I had worked for Doc Sledge, assisting him on barn calls. My important job: holding a cow's head while he worked on the other end.

I beat out a less qualified dental contender by a nose.

Dental training school changed my life, but it wasn't my oral aptitude that set me on a fresh tack.

It was an incident in a stairwell where I almost killed a man.

No Hawaiian sunrise ever lifted my spirits like my Dawn's letters to me mending romantic fences! Embers of love reignited as I left the Islands bound for new training in San Diego, where I began attending Sweetwater Assemblies of God church. I took up residence at barracks near the dental training complex, and I couldn't wait to see Dawn. We arranged for her to stay with friends while she visited me in San Diego. I planned to be an exciting tour guide, thrilling my fiancée with Disneyland and Knots Berry Farm.

Two of my bunkmates who attended dental school with me were civil and friendly, but Lester was not. I tried to ignore Lester's colorful, demeaning remarks about me, figuring I could weather his hateful comments for the remaining 12 weeks. Then Lester's viper tongue flicked on a subject dear to my heart: Dawn.

I informed my commander at the dental school about my fiancée's upcoming visit and that Lester never missed an opportunity to spew vulgarities about Dawn. He even said he had plans for Dawn when she arrived.

"Well, sailor, warn him one more time before you lower the boom."

"Respectfully, *no*, sir. I already warned him."

The seaman dressed in whites pursed his lips for a few seconds, then nodded resignedly. I could tell he was putting himself in my place. "You won't be reprimanded if you take care of this on your own. Dismissed."

I spun on my heel, closed the door and headed for the stairs, where my stomach knotted like a bowline. Lester and two buddies were coming up.

"So, is your b**** coming down this weekend?"

I had contemplated this KO for about three weeks. My fist would plaster Lester's nose on the back of his head, killing him dead.

My agenda didn't belong to Duane, the responsible, the easygoing, the straight-arrow, the churchgoing young man. This was Sailor Steve, who lived deep inside me. (Steve was my given name, but everyone back home called me by my middle name: Duane. The Navy called me Steve.)

My alter-ego, Steve, had never mutinied until today.

Lester handed his books to his friends. He turned his head slightly, spoiling my aim, and my knuckles hammered the edge of his temple. He skipped a couple stairs and landed like a spud sack on the concrete floor.

Lester lay still as death while I stood over him, waiting for … what? Did I think he was getting up? I felt confused as Steve slunk away. Then Duane felt strong arms, and Lester's buddies escorted me to the head man's office, where I had just discussed Lester minutes before.

"If'n the Navy don't get ya', we will."

"One at a time or both of you. Bring it on."

Lester's seconds left me with the exasperated commander. He quizzed me a little, reiterated his promise, then dismissed me.

Lester's doctor told him that if the punch had been a quarter-inch further back on his head, it would have killed him.

I missed a court martial and prison by a quarter of an inch.

Later I met bandaged-up Lester in a locker room, and we both apologized profusely. I bought him a coke and all was forgiven — between us. His friends held the grudge, and I slept with a knife under my pillow until I left dental school.

I determined not to let Steve out of the cellar again, if I wanted to keep from hurting someone. But my alter-ego hated being locked up ...

I was assigned to the USS *Sanctuary* hospital ship — chock full of cavities and bad gums. We sailed for South America, and on shore leave, we sailors were instructed to stick together in port cities, to avoid getting robbed or worse.

A warm camaraderie chipped away at my untested moral fortitude. I was far from Apiary, my father and our little Assemblies of God church. At first, I only sipped at drinks with the guys. I was the trusty sailor who held the winnings at casinos and could help them find the ship when they were stumble-drunk.

"No matter what I say or how I threaten to kick your a**, DON'T give me back my money tonight! Okay?"

My shipmates could depend upon me. It was in my blood to be hard-headed. I earned respect, and it felt right.

Soon in places like Buenaventura, Colombia; Port-au-Prince, Haiti; Panama City, Panama, a sailor's sad playgrounds became mine, too.

My cultural Christian roots lay dormant in my soul, while Steve decided to stay awake drinking Harvey Wallbangers. Steve had few inhibitions when he drank high-octane alcohol and could sing cowboy songs with very little coaxing.

My signature song was "The Auctioneer," and I performed it in bars where few spoke English, and they loved it again and again!

One night at a Colombia nightclub, I sang "Strangers in the Night" with the Elvis of South America, who lit up the stage with an emerald green rhinestone coat. I was stuffed like a tick with aguardientes (firewater), and later Steve wrecked the hotel lobby. My shipmates paid off the hotel manager so they wouldn't call *la policia* and hauled me back to the ship.

I never got off scot-free when I drank. A voice in my heart softly said, *You know this isn't right.*

This time, my body shook like a leaf, and fever roared in my ears. Alcohol poisoning wracked me, and I tossed and turned in a room with 30 sailors who morphed into grotesque shapes. In lucid moments between delirium, I decided to end my debauchery for good.

But months of drinking had changed me. Sadly, my brain told me that being sober wasn't as fun as being intoxicated, and hard liquor filled a *need* in my life. Alcohol was the basis for friendships, song and my sailor's identity. I could never give it up without what my pastor back home called a "deliverance."

"Jesus, I'm so sick and tired of living this way. I need your help."

I had never talked to God this way before, and suddenly Jesus wasn't only my father's God anymore. That night in an iron room aboard ship, Jesus came *close*, and I knew that I owed him my life. How God took away the lust that ruled me I'll never know, but like steam from a boiler, the *need* for alcohol dissipated and was gone.

For most of my friends aboard the *Sanctuary*, our voyage to Haiti included carousing and gambling at dingy casinos. Not for me. I still held my mates' money like a stubborn bank teller, but my nights of club-hopping and drinking were over. I searched out other Christian men aboard ship, and seven of us formed a Bible study group. I was only 21, but they called me their elder because of the knowledge I had soaked up in children's Sunday school back home.

My old-time religion (taken for granted for so many years) was a hot commodity with my Christian shipmates. David and Saul, Peter and Paul came alive in my mind. I taught Bible lessons, and sailors hung onto the words of God like a life preserver.

It was getting close to my discharge when the *Sanctuary* sailed to Naval Station Mayport, at Jacksonville, Florida, and I took my father's advice (for a change) and set out to find a church first thing.

Sweat drizzled down my sides as I waited at a bus stop, and I felt Steve trying to shove his way into my brain. I figured that the church service at Jacksonville Beach would be half over before I arrived.

"Look, God, if the bus isn't here in five minutes, I'm done. I'll just go back to the ship." I glanced at my watch, a little sheepish, trying to regain control.

It wasn't even two minutes before an old white city transport blustered up in a cloud of diesel smoke. I took the only seat available, and a skinny guy beside me introduced himself.

"My name's Bob. Where y'all hayded?" In all my ports of call, I had never heard such a nasally twang.

"Jacksonville Beach Assembly."

"Waaaylll, peeeeeraise the Lord, Brother! I'm on the church board there!"

Coincidence?

Bob introduced me to his friends who even church folks called "Jesus Freaks." Most were hippies, and some were suits and blue-collar men. They mingled like Mom's garden veggies, and working with these unpretentious, wonderful people refreshed my soul. It was like standing on the foredeck on the *Sanctuary* in a Caribbean breeze. I could tell they really loved God.

Bob took me under his wing and taught me how to be a fisher of men, like Jesus' first disciples were. We talked to people about how Jesus had changed us inside, and God landed the ones who were starving for a new life. Bob's sea was the Jacksonville boardwalks, and over the months before my discharge, I became a hardcore street preacher like he was.

Life got sweeter as I thought about my Dawn back home, waiting for me. I knew that Crown Zellerbach held positions open for veterans, and I looked forward to starting a family and sinking roots in the same soil as my father and grandfather.

So, my phone conversation with my mother didn't exactly put a grin on my face.

"Duane. You can't get married just yet."

Her serious tone took me by surprise. "Why, what's wrong?"

"It's too close to my due date, son."

When I arrived home, Apiary seemed to have been frozen in time. Dad still smelled of sawdust, and Mom canned fruits and vegetables in her apron. I moved back into my room for a time, and Dawn and I set a new date for our wedding.

Baby number nine came right on schedule, and Dawn and I were married in August. Dad put in for a little more overtime.

❧❧❧

In the years following my discharge from the Navy, I worked my way off the green chain and enjoyed respect from my co-workers as a saw doctor.

Dawn and I had two beautiful daughters whom we adored. We held a lease option on a beautiful home on acres of pastureland, and I joined a horseback law-enforcement team who rode to rescue missing children or hikers lost in the mountains. Our posse saddled up for parades, leather stirrups creaking and side arms glinting.

I taught adult Sunday school and served on various committees at our Assemblies of God church. The Guisinger families took up even *more* pews now. Rose Fiddler still baked scrumptious pies for folks, but at 91 years old, she seldom attended church anymore.

I savored a respectable position in the Apiary-Rainier community, but sensed an uncomfortable sharpening of purpose inside me, like someone rasped on iron teeth. I loved my deer and elk hunting, and Steve had no problem popping out now and then, knocking down a few deer out of season to fill freezers for the needy. I believed that my .35 Remington answered a higher calling.

Conflicted, yet firmly in God's powerful grip, I wrestled against perceived religious expectations — while yearning to know Jesus as an intimate friend. Studying the Bible became nearly as important to me as hunting! Every verse seemed to come alive, and I prayed more fervently for God to use me as a tool to help others.

One day, I got what I prayed for, without warning.

❧❧❧

Preparing salmon tackle for Kanektok clients had the same calming effect upon my mind as filing circular and band saw teeth at the sawmill.

At sunrise I sat on a log with a cup of coffee, in the Alaska bush — an exile from God's people and purposes. I slapped a liberal dose of bug dope on my neck while I checked over a tackle box full of weights, hooks and lures. The next group of clients would fly in from the tiny airstrip at Quinhagak today.

Dad always figured I'd go haywire, and I sure did ...

Suddenly adrenaline surged from a commotion on the river's surface. We never knew when a grizzly might slosh into camp, and I grabbed at the .44 in my shoulder holster.

I settled back to my log, smiling as three mallards rose from the water, and the thump of wings on the wind took my breath away. Their silhouettes skimmed the late summer horizon, leaving me in deep thought. I felt a piece of my old shame take wing, too, and I bowed my head.

Out of the billions of people on the earth, Jesus and I enjoyed that glorious moment with God's creatures. I know that he did that just for me. God hasn't left me at all.

I had been sending letters to Dawn and the kids (we had four children now) like clockwork, and summer was growing weary, its thick leafy alders and currants smelling musty. My employment as a river guide was ending, and I had no idea what to do when I got back to civilization. Should I find a good state job and work the rest of my life? Or did God still have enough confidence in me to plug me into a pulpit again? The latter seemed unlikely.

During my summer-long therapy as a fishing guide, I noticed some emotional vigor returning to my mind, and in the following days of breaking camp, I retraced my personal path with Jesus, one more time. His unmistakable calling transcended every blunder and triumph, from my boyhood to troubled manhood. It stood out as clearly as Mt. St. Helens against an azure sky.

๖๖๖

GO TO ALASKA, AND GO NOW.

God doesn't call a flawed individual to serve him, does he? Perhaps Jesus didn't know about Steve ...

Yet the call in my heart to sacrifice everything for Jesus' sake was unmistakable.

I asked for signs. I wrangled over throwing away my plum job as a saw doctor at the sawmill. My Guisinger family reputation was on the line: I would lose respect if people heard about my harebrained Far North leap of faith.

Alaska. I had relatives there, and I enjoyed hunting and fishing when we visited, but my *heritage* was rooted in Oregon forests and farms.

My call to Alaska felt like an unrelenting pressure in my chest, gentle but persistent. I woke with it each afternoon; I filed saws with it on my swing shift. How could I leave my life behind — bills, home, family — and just go, without a plan? I could imagine my blueprint for retirement blistering in flames.

I really tried to keep my call to Alaska under wraps as long as possible, but one evening when I was in bed, I lost it. Tears streamed into my pillow, and Dawn sat up.

"Honey! What is it?"

I snuffled a bit and finally blurted out, "God is telling me to go to Alaska, and go NOW. I have no idea exactly where I'm going or when I'll be back."

Silence.

"Dawn?"

"Okay."

"Okay?"

"Hon, we'll be alright. Do what God is telling you."

Resigning from my church responsibilities troubled me, and my father just shook his head as I announced my intentions to the congregation. Where was my common sense?

Driving home after the service, I passed Rose Fiddler's house, and I suddenly felt like God was topping off my tank with another message: *Rose has something to tell you — then I can take her home.*

Lord?

This was too much to handle. Steve stepped on the accelerator, steamed about all the unnatural counsel he was getting. It made me look downright weird!

I regained control, whipped around and pulled into Rose's driveway.

"Ah, Mr. Guisinger ..." Sister Fiddler stood all of 4 feet tall in the dimly lit doorway — and she thought she was talking to my father.

Great ...

When I explained who I *really* was, she invited me inside.

I was running scared now, worried that she would drop dead immediately after giving me some godly advice. I nervously filled up our conversation, until she excused herself for a moment to go to the kitchen. I really didn't want any pie …

Returning with a heavy blue mixing bowl, she placed it in my hands. "Duane, if I don't use this bowl every time I make my pies, they aren't worth a continental." Sister Fiddler's eyes flashed like fire. "God's telling you that YOU are the mixing bowl for Alaska, and you're needed right now."

No pie tonight. I hurried out the door, hoping I outdistanced inevitable Providence.

I tried to explain to my dad about my illogical call from God, and he used his fatherly power of persuasion to jam a board in my gears. I should postpone my Alaska trip until June, when I could take the family and make it a vacation … I could work enough overtime to save up for the trip. It was the only sane, reasonable decision.

Wasn't he right? I could still obey God, but just tweak the timetable a bit.

Then, at Crown Zellerbach's main gate, Lonny, the security guard, helped me cinch the deal. He was wearing a cocky half smile. "What're you doing here, Guisinger?"

I wasn't in any mood for banter, and Steve wanted to grab him. "I work here, remember?"

"Not anymore. The mill's closing …"

I called home and told Dawn to pack my bags for Alaska.

Crown Zellerbach in Rainier never officially reopened again.

In Alaska, I never figured I'd be interrogated by an FBI agent. I sat in a room in downtown Anchorage, dressed in Levis and cowboy boots, with a year's growth of beard and longish hair — waiting for a verdict.

To be approved would take another miracle.

I had slept the night as a guest of an Alaska missionary family who picked me up at the airport. These gracious people knew my relatives, and they were my only link to Anchorage. They suggested that I spend some time at Teen Challenge, to make connections for employment.

Everything suddenly shifted into high gear when the Teen Challenge executive director, Merle, asked me to take a ride with him to Palmer. We looked over a new Teen Challenge housing site and got to know one another.

He chewed on my story, evaluating me, all the way back to Anchorage — and suddenly Merle asked me pointblank: "Do you want to serve as our new director over men's housing?"

My heart leaped. I didn't hesitate.

"Good. We can meet with the board of directors in a few hours, to get their go-ahead."

The three directors of the board for Teen Challenge Alaska were all dressed fit to kill.

The man asking all the questions worked for the FBI, too, and he knew all the right buttons to push to discover my true heart.

At the end of the interview, everyone was in agreement. They had their man. In fact, they had been praying for seven months for a men's director and worked on a tight deadline. God met the deadline with only hours to spare. I was their answer to prayer, and it felt wonderful!

I flew home with answers for everyone who had doubted my call. I hoped to sit down and hold Rose Fiddler's frail hands, acknowledging her prophetic encouragement — but I had to leave that with God. Sister Fiddler had lapsed into a comatose condition days after I left for Alaska. In fact, I was the last person she ever ministered to.

Our Rose passed away, and I cherished her memorial service, a milepost that reconfirmed my call to preach after my dark days of doubting.

One more peculiar obstacle remained for me to hurdle before I moved the family to Alaska, lock, stock and barrel. I was tying up loose ends and had hitched a ride to Alaska to secure a place for Dawn and the kids. She was supportive and seemed convinced that we were on the right track.

I worked for much of the summer at a Soldotna grocery store, waiting for the official word to move into Teen Challenge housing — and once in a while, Steve showed up to distract me. One day he pointed out how much my knees hurt. My hands were cut up from cardboard boxes, and I worried that I hadn't heard back from Merle, the Teen Challenge executive director.

In the breakfast food aisle, I told God, "You called me to Alaska, I know, but here I am stocking shelves! Look at that, Lord! A box of Cheerios has a higher position than me."

I knew when I said it that God was shining a spotlight — right at Steve.

You are called to be a servant, not someone with a position.

My call felt solid. But God was peeling a prideful self-sufficiency from me, a little at a time. It would take nearly a decade to teach me how utterly dependent I was on Jesus.

The same week that I had this Cheerios epiphany, I received the phone call I had been praying for. "Duane, can you start work at Teen Challenge in 30 days?" This meant that my family would have a residence, and I would be working in the ministry that God had called me to!

I said yes. I had my plane ticket, and I would be leaving that very night to pack up and move my family north.

But a second phone call 60 minutes later set me back on my heels. It was the *brand-new* executive director of Teen Challenge, who had replaced Merle.

"I hear that you are heading back to Oregon to move your family up, is that right?" Joe had a New York accent, and I pictured him looking like a little mafia don.

"Yes, sir. I have it all worked out with Merle."

"Are you under the impression that you have a permanent position at Teen Challenge?"

Dead silence.

"Yes, sir. I absolutely am under that impression." An avalanche of emotions broke loose, and Steve woke up.

"Mr. Guisinger, I need you to know that nothing has been promised."

I had much more to say that couldn't be articulated over the telephone — but I made a stab at illuminating the new director. To my surprise, he seemed understanding.

"I'll meet you at the airport before you fly out to Oregon. We'll talk."

A few hours later, I sat with a cup of strong coffee in the airport lobby, awaiting the man who had the power to cast my reputation in a dumpster or confirm my call to Alaska. Preserving honor and character had been branded upon my brain since childhood, and I treasured my independence. People knew me as a man of my word. A powerful, God-fearing man, respected, steady, reliable … to be humbled by this New Yorker stuck in my craw! He could ruin everything! In Apiary, I would be a laughing stock.

The new director, Joe, looked just like I pictured him, but when he extended his hand the unexpected happened — I loved the guy, like a best friend. Merle was with him, and in less than an hour, Joe felt the same as Merle about me. We ambled toward my boarding gate, and I finally asked, "What do I tell my people back home, Joe? Do I have the job?"

"Duane, how would you like to be our new Teen Challenge training center director?"

"You mean over the whole shootin' match?"

"That's right. Over our training center here in Alaska."

Thirty days later, Dawn mopped a foreign kitchen and unpacked our lives into just two bedrooms alongside rooms that would soon fill with broken men and women needing Jesus.

For years, I ran a marathon that never had a finish line. I focused every ounce of my emotional, physical and spiritual strength on never-ending tasks that I believed God expected me to complete.

If anyone had warned me to strike a gentle pace, to delight in the beauty of Alaska, to savor my family and relationships, I would have been too burdened with *achieving for Jesus* to listen.

I ministered to men and women addicted to drugs and alcohol. I helped teach them how to live God-centered lives based upon a personal relationship with Jesus. Some were under orders by the court to remain with us for a year or more, and I became a third-party custodian or probation officer for many. In some cases, I had the authority by law to decide when they could be released into society.

I received ministerial credentials with the Assemblies of God, and a Christian brother blessed me with a fully paid trip to Israel and Egypt. I traveled to Europe and Africa on a mission trip, and I was proud that people called me Pastor Duane — a faith-walker and an example of livin' right.

At the end of eight years as a Teen Challenge administrator, pastor and counselor, as well as a board member, musician and teacher at a local church, my self-sufficient 24/7 lifestyle had *weakened* me.

I moved the family to a small community farther north and headed into ministry at my usual dead run — and that's where I hit the wall. I loved my new people, but my spiritual gumption was all dried up. I stumbled — and fell.

We moved back to Wasilla, and charitable friends took us in, giving us a basement apartment to live in while I tried to find employment. For months, every door slammed in my face, until one day I just stopped looking. I lay in the dark, wanting God to kill me, while my children and Dawn clattered morning dishes before school.

I remembered an embarrassing story my mother once told me about me trying to dig up Grandfather Archibald at his graveside service. I missed Grandpa, and in my 3-year-old mind, I hoped to rescue him.

Now in my 40s, I wanted to join him. I heard the door slam; happy children's voices faded, and all was silent, like Grandpa's grave.

Suddenly the bedroom door opened, and irritating light flooded the room. My wife stood beside me, staring at me. I suffocated in failure and couldn't move, until her voice, like a spurt of oxygen, reached deep into my spirit. She had left her heritage behind, too, and I recalled all the times I abandoned her to care for home and children while I worked for God.

Even now, as I wallowed in self-pity, she stood beside me. So when she spoke, I listened, knowing her words came from God.

"Duane … aren't you even going to try?"

It wasn't a reprimand; it was a plea. And something that I believed was long dead reached out to Dawn. My beautiful wife saved my life that morning.

I made Dawn a promise to try again — a hollow promise at best, but Jesus was listening. I got dressed for the first time in days.

Some might call my giving up on life a breakdown. But I see it as a breakup — the shattering of a case-hardened ego handed down from generations of self-made men, as far back as Adam, the first man God ever created. God allowed my self-centered way of serving Jesus to reach its end.

❧❧❧

"I hear you're looking for work. You wanna job guiding fishermen in the bush? You'd be gone for a few months, working about 90 miles south of Bethel, near the Yup'ik village of Quinhagak."

It was the one thing that I felt confident I could still do: *fish*. So about a week after my promise to Dawn, I was setting up bunks in portable huts, clearing brush and organizing tackle to help well-heeled city dudes catch a big one. My clients and I never suffered a single fishless day the whole summer.

It was during these months of convalescence on the Kanektok River that I threw off my shame like a sweat-soaked backpack. I realized that Jesus never asked me to carry it at all.

I gave up control of decisions and every detail affecting my future — even the ones the size of a no-see-um's eyelash.

After I got home, all tanned and uncertain, I hugged Dawn and my beloved children, emptied of pride and on the trail of regaining my strength of mind.

It took another three years to rekindle the home fires — taking a job as a security guard, spending time with my children and rebuilding my relationship with Dawn. We were attending a church where I taught adult Sunday school and served on the board, when my pastor and friend posed a challenge.

"Duane, I'm worn out. Can you help me conduct services at Sunny Knik Chapel? I need someone who can preach every other Sunday."

Pastor had been traveling 22 miles each way, ministering to a small flock of faithful people until they found a permanent pastor. Cautiously and prayerfully, I agreed to fill in, never dreaming that Jesus would reignite my call to ministry through the precious ones at Sunny Knik.

After a few months of visiting, leading worship in song and teaching these folks, they became as close as family.

Jesus reminded me that I could not unring a bell — even in my darkened basement, God's calling had never been extinguished. My strange Alaskan odyssey had prepared me to love and serve my brothers and sisters at Sunny Knik.

I became their pastor more than 15 years ago.

࿇࿇࿇

In Alaska, nothing strikes fear in a puny human being like the emotionless eyes of a grizzly. His expression conveys one simple message: YOU ARE PREY.

Three times in recent years I have experienced this kind of helpless feeling, staring death in the eyes, but two instances were from sudden illnesses — not from a brownie killer.

The year that I helped re-launch Sunny Knik Chapel as a part-time minister, my knee suddenly grew infected with toxic strep, and I gave my doctor permission to amputate my leg, if it would save my life. He skillfully scraped the inside clean of infection, and for days I hovered between life and heaven with a 106-degree fever.

But my soul wasn't in the hospital at all. I lay in a cave where God was communicating with me. War raged outside, and a burly angel stood beside me. He held a great curved sword with a phrase engraved on the blade: "The Will and Power of God."

I roused three days later with an indelible picture of my life — where I had been and where I was going. I had given the enemy, Satan, the upper hand in years past, because of my selfish pride, but Jesus had rescued me by permitting the enemy to overpower me for a time. I had learned from the experience and was ready for the rest of the battle.

For now, God removed me from the fight, and I would reenter the battle refreshed.

I recovered fully, and in a matter of weeks, Jesus swept me into the ministry at Sunny Knik.

પ્ર���

During some of my most fulfilling years as a pastor at Sunny Knik, I stared into the eyes of the beast again.

After weeks of passing blood, my doctor ordered a biopsy, and it came back positive for cancer in my bladder area. On September 11, 2001, my nephew-in-law drove me to the mountains so that I could pray and make my peace with the ordeal ahead. I stood in the mountains near Eureka, asking God to heal me.

What if my cancer spread? Would I become bedridden, like so many cancer victims I had visited over the years?

"Lord, this is a real nuisance!" I said, feeling Steve rising up. I quickly gave Jesus control of my situation again. "Okay. You know what I want, but your will be done, Lord."

When I got into cell range, I called my wife to tell her I was on my way home.

"Duane! Have you heard about the attack on the Twin Towers in New York?"

Suddenly my own problem seemed miniscule compared to wounds suffered by my nation.

My physician, Dr. Crandall, burned away the lumps in my bladder before my second biopsy came back from the lab. While I lay in recovery, sore and restless, Dr. Crandall came in, and I noted a peculiar concern on his face.

"Duane, I have your second biopsy results." He paused, looking at the chart again just to make sure he was reading it right. "Remember how your first biopsy showed cancer? Your second biopsy ..." Dr. Crandall waved the clipboard, "your second biopsy shows no sign of cancer. We operated for no reason!"

I laughed carefully, mindful of some pain. "Looks like Jesus helped you out there, Doc."

In the following months, doctors and nurses were amazed that my bladder healed up completely normal, as if no cancer had ever been detected.

᳕᳕᳕

Stress can kill a preacher as dead as any grizzly can — so I fish, hunt or tramp the wilderness to let off steam whenever I have time. In the mountains or sitting on riverbanks, Jesus reminds me of his control and authority over every mosquito, volcano and over this old pastor, too.

After a bout of pneumonia a few years ago, I noticed a little weakness in my legs as I tracked a moose through a draw at the bottom of a ridge. My son-in-law rode his four-wheeler hunting the top of the saddleback, but my trail was a little too narrow for me to ride mine.

We hunted with .50-caliber muzzle loaders: single-shot black powder rifles, the only legal gun for this moose hunt. Finally, about a mile from my four-wheeler, I turned around wearily — with no sign of my moose steaks.

The draw suddenly looked familiar. I had killed a black bear at this exact spot some time ago, and I mused: *I'd hate to meet a brownie in all this brush right now ...*

I figure that the old boar grizzly and I must have been hunting the same moose, because he looked as surprised as I, barreling down the draw right for me. Maybe with his little pig eyes, I looked like a moose to him.

I had left my trusty .44 pistol back at the pickup truck (it was too cotton-pickin' heavy to pack on a hike), so I raised my old-timey rifle, sighting through the flying clods of snow, throat-fog and directly into galloping brown fur.

"Lord, help this thing to go off ..." I needed to scare him or kill him — or I was finished.

The bear was 10 yards from me when my gun's *snap-boom!* echoed against the ridge. I blinked away white smoke, while the dying grizzly thrashed, grabbing and biting at everything he could find.

As he lumbered into the brush and disappeared, I shook my head, breathing, "Thanks, Lord. I appreciate it."

It took a little time for me to drop powder down the long octagon barrel of my muzzle loader and follow up with a patch and ball. My whole body shook from cold and sheer adrenaline. I started after the old grizzly, hoping to make sure he was dead, but I never did locate him, as snowy and dark as it was.

No doubt, God saved me once again for his purposes.

These days, Dawn and I enjoy a precious heritage more enduring than any we knew in the shadow of Mt. St. Helens. Our roots grow deep at Sunny Knik, twining with elders and youngsters in soil tended by God himself. New friends move to our neck of the woods every week, and our corral is about full these days.

We anticipate miracles, serving a multitude of Alaskans, as Jesus multiplies every penny like fishes and every moment of time like nourishing bread.

CONCLUSION

It is never easy to stay the course. It can seem impossible to recover, to be rescued, to be saved.

A verse of a long-loved hymn states:

"I was sinking deep in sin, far from the peaceful shore. Very deeply stained within, sinking to rise no more. But the Master of the sea heard my despairing cry. From the waters lifted me, now safe am I. Love lifted me! Love lifted me! When nothing else could help, Love lifted me!"

As we were preparing these stories, I was asked to conduct a memorial service for a very beautiful young woman. A young woman who had struggled and lost the fight of life against the tides that dragged her down. Hopeless and overwhelmed, she slipped into eternity. She did not have to lose. There was another answer. There is a God who would have given her love, joy, hope, peace and so much more.

This book was made available to you to let you know that YOU do not have to sink! God sees your situation and he cares. He is standing ready to take your hand, to change your life and your destiny.

There is real hope! It is found in the person of Jesus Christ. We here at Sunny Knik Chapel would love the opportunity to help you know more about the love that God offers. As you have read, not one of us is perfect, and none of us have room to condemn others. We carry scars in body and soul. Some have healed, and some are still healing. We are no strangers to the hurting and searching soul. You CAN experience peace of mind and spirit. You can know newness of life and freedom.

Jesus once reached out his hand to a desperate and drowning man named Simon Peter. That very same loving hand reached out to each of these seven storytellers. And now, this same Jesus is reaching out his hand to you. Right now, right where you are, just as you are. TAKE HOLD OF THAT HAND! The Bible tells us in 2 Corinthians 5:17 that if we take hold of that hand (believe in him and ask him to guide our lives), he makes us new! "Therefore if any man be in Christ, he is a new creature: old things are passed away; behold, all things are become new" (KJV). The old things of life are now gone and forgiven. Christ is now making all things new! He provides the freedom to truly live!

Some of you reading this may have, at one time, asked Jesus to be a part of your life. Perhaps you have read the Bible and have even gone to church. Maybe you've been a leader or a minister in the church and, like Simon Peter, have found yourself sinking. You, too, can be rescued. Whatever it was that caused you to start sinking, it doesn't matter. Jesus has never stopped loving you. He is willing to forgive you. He wants to restore your life and heal your hurts. He has promised that he will make all things new! You may have failed or others may have failed you, but hear me, God NEVER fails. He has not given up on you! Enter into the joy of the living, loving and forgiving Christ!

CONCLUSION

Whether you've never asked Jesus to come into your life or you've been walking with him for ages and have simply fallen out of touch, the answer is the same: TAKE HOLD OF HIS HAND!

To take his hand, simply talk to Jesus and say these words:

Lord, help me! I really am sinking. Jesus, I am reaching for your hand. Forgive every bad thing I've done and every failure. Create in me this new life promised to anyone who calls out to you. Thank you for loving me even when I feel completely unlovable. Thank you for reaching out to me! Lord, please help me as I walk through this life. Help me to love you and to love others. I believe you will do what you've promised. Amen.

If you were sincere in that prayer, God is already at work! I would encourage you to start reading the Bible. If you don't have one, we would love to give you one. A great place to start is in the Gospel of John. Also, start talking with Jesus every day. It doesn't have to be intimidating, just talk to him like you would to a close friend. Know that you are not alone. Find a good Jesus-loving, Bible-teaching group of believers (a church) where you can learn and grow with the help of a loving and caring group of people who have gone through stuff just like you. We invite you to come and check us out at Sunny Knik Chapel.

PERILOUS TIDES

What an awesome relief to know that we can now, because of Christ, sail above life's Perilous Tides.

We will be looking for you on Sunday!

S. Duane Guisinger
Pastor of Sunny Knik Chapel
Knik, Alaska

We would love for you to join us at Sunny Knik Chapel!

We meet Sunday mornings at 10 a.m. at
Mile 14 Knik-Goose Bay Road
Knik, Alaska 99654.

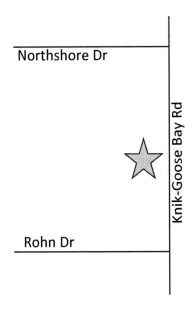

For more information or directions,
please contact us at 907.376.8777.

For more information on reaching your city with
stories from your church, please contact
Good Catch Publishing at
www.goodcatchpublishing.com

GOOD CATCH
PUBLISHING

Did one of these stories touch you?
Did one of these real people move you to tears?
Tell us (and them) about it on our reader blog at
www.goodcatchpublishing.blogspot.com.